To Rev. Voe

Thanks for your interest

In The Carpenter's Workshop

Volume 1

An Exploration Of The Use Of Drama In Story Sermons

Jerry Eckert

Jerry Eckert

5-24-97

CSS Publishing Company, Inc., Lima, Ohio

Library of Congress Cataloging-in-Publication Data

Eckert, Jerry O., 1935
    In the Carpenter's workshop : an exploration of the use of drama in story sermons /
Jerry O. Eckert.
        p.   cm.
    ISBN 0-7880-0760-2
    1. Story sermons. 2. Methodist Church—Sermons. 3. Sermons, American. I. Title.
BV4307.S7E34   1997
252—dc20   96-38672
                                                                        CIP

This book is available in the following formats, listed by ISBN:
    0-7880-0760-2   Book
    0-7880-0892-7   MAC
    0-7880-0893-5   IBM 3 1/2
    0-7880-0894-3   Sermon Prep

This little book is dedicated to Bill Hienz and the rest of the Faith Players of Faith United Methodist Church, Milwaukee, Wisconsin.

Bill was the first person to encourage me to write down these story sermons in the form of a book, and Bill was the first to say yes when I asked for help to do one of the dramatization sermons illustrated here. His and my colleagues in the Players groups deserve much of the credit for this experience coming to flower for, without a wide variety of people to lean upon, the variety of alternative formats would have been limited.

Table Of Contents

Foreword

The use of storytelling as a medium for the sermon is not new. Many books, seminary professors, and preachers have been using techniques like writing letters from the point of view of a biblical character, or using short story formats to get their message across.

This first of three little volumes does some of that, but takes this technique a step further.

During my ministry, I was appointed to a church that had a drama group. "Drama" may overstate their gift as performers. They put on such plays as "Some of My Best Friends Are Spies" and "Penelope, Pride of the Pickle Factory." Having done some story sermons in previous years, I decided to take a chance. I dramatized some of my sermons by varying my own voicing so that I literally played the parts of some of the characters in my story sermons. The congregation was not critical of me. In fact, I was encouraged to put them into a book.

With such support, I took the next step, preparing texts for the story sermons which included lines for people in the congregation. The first such effort was a telling of the story of the Tower of Babel using "You Are There," the CBS radio and television format, as the model.

That Sunday morning, I handed out scripts to about eight folks when they came in the door. These were mostly members of the drama group. They picked up on it right away, scanned their scripts during the early part of the service, and were ready to go when it was time for the sermon. I left the pulpit, taking along the lavaliere microphone, and went from person to person where they sat in the pews. The people did strikingly well. One of the treats for me was giving them the good lines, something I tried to do in nearly all the rest of my efforts.

While the collection will seem large by the time the third volume is before you, please note the dates. This collection constitutes about one fourth of the sermons I preached in that church and only a twentieth of what I did in my last two churches. I used the traditional sermonic formats most of the other times.

I have included some because I'm very proud of them. Most are included as samples of the variety of possibilities. I sincerely hope that these sermons will not be used as they are in your churches. The best sermons are the ones which grow out of the life of a congregation and its needs. The best "drama" story sermons can really only grow out of the level of the talents of the local church.

Introduction

More scholarly work than this has traced the use of drama and story telling in the life of the Church. What you have here and in the following two volumes is an existential exploration: what happened, when it happened, how it happened, in the experience of one who found the circumstances coming together to experiment with them in local churches.

No claims are here made for profundity, no more than can be found as a person goes through life a day at a time, doing the daily things. This is not to say that there can be no depth. The listener may see well beyond what even the most profound visionaries offer. Here, the attempt is made to set the congregation in the midst of an event. Each is faithful to the biblical story, exceptions being noted. In trying to make the event seem authentic, there is the difficult problem of adding detail that fills out the sparse scriptural telling. There will be some for whom this writer's choice of particulars will be offensive. Hopefully, that will inspire them to attempt this task to provide their own detail and be original in their own right.

The purpose here is to give the listener/reader of these augmented stories a sense of the life issues faced and some possible models with whom to identify and from whom to learn.

You will note that despite all the inherent preaching, there are not that many attempts to "explain" the stories. Most people get a bigger thrill out of figuring out something for themselves than they do having everything laid out for them, at least on the first and third Sundays of the month. The second and fourth, they would just as soon have someone do their thinking for them! Life is too hard to do your own thinking all the time!

The occasional use of drama-enhanced sermons may be one technique pastors and preachers can add to their tool box. It is something other laity with the gifts for drama can consider in opportunities they may have to proclaim the gospel. The Word of God is a living Word, not a scholastic entity best treated by lecture format, nor a set of formulae that need to be repeated verbatim! Not only does the Word need to be expressed in the context of human interaction; it needs a variety of humans interacting in the presentation.

Comment: "Why don't you do sermons as stories?" my wife suggested. "You tell stories well and people seem to like them. Besides, you won't end up criticizing us as often!"

My wife has a way about her.

That was all I needed to try it out. Who wants to be preached at? I surely didn't!

The first time I tried the following sermon in its current format, I served a church which had a lay person who had taken university level courses in Old Testament. How do you preach to someone with that kind of background, someone who has as good or better a background than yourself? You tell the story as story and try to let its implications preach themselves in the mind of the listeners. It's hard not to preach, though!

In The Beginning
Genesis 1

"In the beginning God created the heavens and the earth. The earth was without form and void, and darkness was upon the face of the deep...."

It was Sunday when everything began. Everything seems to fall apart on Sundays. Sure, it's nice to not have to go to work, but there is no routine to order our day. All the things we have put off are piled around us and we hardly know where to start, if we have any energy in the first place. For many of us working people, it can be the loneliest day of the week. We miss the likelihood of contact with the people we see daily. Not all of us have family to fill our lives on a weekend. At least with the mess, there is the possibility of something to do, like clean it up!

Whatever that mess was, it was tossing and crashing and twisting and pulling and pushing and, worst of all, it was dark. God was having a hard time with it. He studied it. He felt it. Yes, He felt it. In His face it was smashing and swirling. It pulled at His legs to draw Him down. It tore at His arms to weaken Him. It pounded at His heart to depress Him.

"Enough of this," He cried out. "I can't even see what's going on here. Let there be light!"

Bingo, there was light. Who knows where the switch was? Or who turned it on? Probably one of those voice-activated things with which you can turn on the light when you walk in the room.

That's silly.

It was God who wanted the light. He brought it to play on the tumult by realizing He was in the dark about what was going on.

The darkness fell away and God could see the mess now.

It didn't go away! It kept on pummeling Him, but He was beginning to understand what was going on.

"Hey, this is better. This is good."

God was fascinated. In the dark, He was feeling lost, alone, almost out of it. In the light, He felt so much better about what He was dealing with. He could begin to pick out the currents and swells and eddies and tides in the swirling waters.

"Just trying to get a hold of all this is wearing me out," God said, so He decided to sleep on it. "What is tomorrow for?" He figured. "It doesn't all have to be done today."

The second day was a Monday. Still a lonely day for a loving one like God, and most of the week ahead of Him! But there was His mess, still going at it. Crashing, moving, swaying, enveloping.

"And God said, 'Let there be a firmament in the midst of the waters, and let it separate the waters from the waters.' "

If you have a problem, make smaller problems out of it. Divide and conquer. Take it a little at a time. God was no dummy!

Firmament. That's a dome. Above the spherical roof He made was half the swirling waters. The other half swelled at His feet as He stood admiring His handiwork.

"I've divided it, but the mess is still there. I hope I haven't goofed up the children's curiosity by leaving too easy an answer to their questions about why the sky is blue and where does the rain come from."

God noticed that the dome did not prevent the waters above and the waters below from breaking through occasionally and trying to overcome Him. But there was some peace and order now. And it was time to start thinking about where He was going to put His beings, His creatures, His companions.

God went to bed Monday night not sure His work was all that good that day.

A good night's rest and God was raring to go! Tuesday had barely started and God was out giving orders.

"Let the waters under the heavens be gathered into one place and let dry land appear."

That's what happened. One of the reasons the water was such a mess was because it was full of stuff. And some of that stuff was dirt. When He got a good bunch of that sifted out of the water, He realized He had done a brilliant thing. Now He had three kinds of places for His fellow beings and not just one. He could make all kinds! Some for the land, some for the water, and some for the … air, that's right!

"This is great," God said.

That hadn't taken long, so God tackled something else. Tuesdays can be like that!

"Let the earth put forth vegetation …" God said.

And the plants and their seeds developed all over the place. There were different kinds for different places on the land and in the water and in the air. Not so many up there. Most of those went and hung on trees and were happy.

"I like all My plants where they are," God said. "They're good! Hope no one puts them in the wrong place. I made them with My love, but I made them out of the chaotic stuff in the water!"

"Can't be time for bed already," God said, but time passes for Him, too. Sorry about that.

Wednesday was there almost before He realized it. "Got to do something to take the load off me," He said. He looked the situation over, thought about what He wanted to spend His time doing, and made a decision. There were some things He just wasn't going to have to look after all the time. Like switching the light off and on.

"Let there be lights in the firmament of the heavens to separate the day from the night."

Easier said than done! He had to search long and hard for the stuff in the water to clump together to make the sun and the stars. By the time He got to making the moon, He just collected more dirt and put it up there where it could reflect the sunlight at night.

"Nice touch," He said. He liked it. "Tomorrow, the fun begins," He said, forgetting His loneliness among the plants, and easing pressure on Himself by giving some of His creation a chance to help.

It was Thursday already! Time really flies when you are having fun.

"Let's start out with the critters that will be most at home in the water anyway," God said. Gotta start someplace when it comes to the animals. When things get complicated, pick the easier projects first. Go to the harder ones later when you have had some success and are feeling more confident.

"Now the birds," God said.

"Hey, that was hard work," God said. "Can't spend all my time making critters. Make yourselves, you all!" God shouted. "And do it with My blessing!"

"Got a problem," God said. "How can all these critters keep going without food? I sure haven't got time to go out there and scrounge enough food out of the waters to keep them going, not if I got other things to do. I know! They can help each other out. The birds can eat some of the seeds and plant some of the others for the plants. And the fish can eat some of the plants and then, when they die, they can be fertilizer for the plants. That way they can help keep each other going!"

"What a big day!" God thought. "But watch what I do tomorrow," He said to His air, His land, His plants and their seeds, His fish and His birds, and their babies. "You all are beautiful! But there is more to come."

Friday dawned, thanks to His sun. God stretched Himself. Some pretty sore muscles. He's been working so hard to put this world together. Anybody thinks it's easy has another think coming! Work hasn't changed much, has it!?

"Okay, here we go," God said. And He spoke, and from the stuff of the waters and the land and the air came forth animals, some wild to live on their own and some tame so that they could live with God's next creatures. "I like it!" God said.

"Now let's make some helpers to protect and cherish all the creatures I have made." But remembering His own loneliness, God made two kinds of helpers that would be able to live together and reproduce and love and protect and cherish His Creation. God made men and women.

"It's all yours," God said. "Enjoy, appreciate, celebrate, anticipate, care for it all. Even though it is made of the stuff of chaos, it is formed by My love, for all of you together. And you, My people, are not only part of it, but, like Me, have your work cut out to maintain it in safety and in blessing."

"What could be better?" God said as He looked out over everything that evening as the sun was setting and the moon was rising.

Now if He could only figure out a way to prevent the chaos from breaking out all over. That was something He couldn't entirely pass on to His creation. That was going to take a very long time!

But it was time to rest. In fact, take the day off. "The body needs a rest and the mind needs some time to think about things," God said. So on Saturday, God laid around.

If God can do that, maybe we can take off a day a week ourselves! Sure need the rest! And if we forgot what we were here to be doing, we can sure use the reminding!

Genesis 2:5 begins, "In the day that the Lord God made the earth and the heavens ..." but let's not go into that. That's another story!

Comment: Narrative depends on imagination. Imagination can be triggered by vivid words, by the conversational tone that frees it to flow naturally, by dramatic intonations lending emotion to the intellectual content being offered, and by specific directions to the listeners.

The following sermon was done using the device of directing the congregation to imagine a specific setting, a stage with scenery and props described. The device was reinforced by having the people in the congregation close their eyes and bow their head at the end of each act, and raise their heads and open their eyes at the beginning of the next act.

Anyone who has been to an Avery and Marsh worship service knows that this is not asking too much of a congregation! In fact, a simple physical act that requires only a small amount of energy and does not impinge on modesty usually adds to the enjoyment of the Sunday service by the parishioners.

Adam And Eve And God
Genesis 2-3

There are two stories of the creation in the opening chapters of Genesis. The story from those who live by the sea tells of how God created the heavens and the earth by water and the Word.

The second story, the one we will see today, is from those who live in the desert and tells of how we not only have feet of clay but are of the very essence of dirt from head to toe.

To share this story, let's pretend we are in a theater. I ask that you bow your heads when the curtains close and raise them again when they open. To add to the power of that moment, close your eyes at the closing of the curtains and open them for the new act before you. Some of you may in fact find it helpful to leave your eyes closed in order to see better the stage and its props. If you happen to fall asleep, sweet dreams!

Imagine now the curtains of a stage before you. Close your eyes.

Now open them as the curtains open. Center stage is the lonely figure of God, standing in the midst of sand dunes. The wind is blowing wisps of sand here and there. He stoops down, takes a handful of the reddish soil, and lets it fall through His fingers back onto the stage. He says "Adam" which, in ancient Hebrew, means "red dirt."

Then God raises His hand. As He does so, a mist arises from the ground and waters the whole stage of dunes beginning at His feet. He kneels down when the ground at His feet is wet. With the swift hands of a potter, He forms a red sandy lump into the figure of a man. He stands the figure upright beside Him. The mist falls on it and it does not crumble. God smiles.

He pinches the nostrils of the figure and blows into its mouth. He lets go and the man's eyes open. God steps over to him and embraces him. "Adam," God says. In modern Hebrew, that means "human being."

18

The hug feels good to the man and he smiles. He never heard of homosexuality or having to be macho so the hug doesn't bother him. It simply feels good.

The misty rain stops as it reaches the edge of the stage. Deftly, God builds trees, plants, shrubs, bushes, and all kinds of vegetation of the wet crimson soil. These He touches and they turn bright green. He smiles, and fruits and vegetables form on the plants.

He takes Adam through the newly made garden and gives him directions on how to guard and cultivate it.

"Enjoy," God says with gusto.

"Except for these two trees," He says more quietly, but very distinctly. "You have a choice. I urge that you do not eat of either of them. If you do, life as you know it here will end." God's look is very serious.

Adam shrugs his shoulders, says, "Okay," and goes to work in the garden.

The work is exhilarating and their friendship warm. But Adam doesn't seem to be quite alive yet.

"How are you doing?" God asks.

"Just fine. Couldn't have things any better." Adam is not as convincing as he means to be. Who wants to hurt God's feelings!?

But God, being new at relating to a human being, isn't quite sure what to do. This man needs something more. So God calls upon the mist again and soon is molding and designing and shaping. He calls Adam over. "Help me name these new creatures," He offers.

God touches a small four-legged crouching figure. It springs to life, a green reptilian leaper.

"How about 'frog' for that one?" Adam asks. "Why not?" God replies.

As God touches each of His new creations and it comes to life, Adam pulls a name out of the air. One creature is quite large and gray. Heavy, too. Its legs are as big around as Adam's whole body. Its tail is tiny. So are its ears. Its huge barrel-shaped body looks monstrous. God leads it over into a pond where its heaviness no longer causes it trouble. It moves easily in the water.

"What shall we call this one?" God asks Adam.

"Hippopotamus," Adam responds immediately.

"Hippopotamus?" God is surprised. "How come you want to call it that?"

"Because it looks like one," Adam says.

Adam sparks up, now that he has the animals. No question, God has found companions that Adam can enjoy. The animals romp with him in the cool of the early morning. They surround him at supper time when they all eat together. They curl up together in the midst of the garden when it is time to sleep.

Adam is fine ... for a while. But he begins to droop again.

"Adam," God calls to him. "I see you are happy with the animals, the plants, and Me. But there is still an empty place in your life."

In the middle of the garden on our stage, with the animals watching, God gently touches Adam on the forehead and Adam lies down and falls into a deep sleep. Instead of using the mist and red soil, God reaches into Adam's side, removes a rib, and then, with His marvelous touch, produces on the spot another human being, a woman.

God blows into her mouth, and then touches Adam to wake him. The two humans look up, see each other, and with the innocence of children, reach out and touch each other. And that feels very good.

"In Myself, I am complete," God says, "but now I realize you are not. Together, you will be complete."

And they are. Adam takes his new companion, shows her the whole garden, introduces her to all the animals, shows her what work needs to be done, and hands her a hoe. When they are done, she hands him some fruit to peel for supper, while she makes some wheat cakes. And they are happy. The animals make room for them as the sun begins to set. They snuggle down for the night and find their completeness. The animals don't mind.

The curtain closes and we bow our heads, close our eyes, with the end of act one.

Act two, the curtain opens, as do our eyes. At center stage are all the trees of the garden. Eve, alone, is walking among them, taking a coffee break. As she comes to one of those God has said was off limits, a very slender figure, about her height, slips out from behind it and engages her in a little conversation. Not only can they talk to God face to face, they can talk to the animals.

"Did God tell you to s-s-stay away from all thes-s-se trees-s-s?" the slender one asks.

"Only this one. And we dasn't even touch it or we'll die," she replies. That's not exactly what God said. Close.

"You won't die," the snaky fellow says. "You will only become wis-s-se like God, being able to dec-c-cide for yours-s-self what is-s-s good and bad. You will notic-c-ce everything! But you won't die," he adds quickly.

Hesitantly, she reaches up for one of the fruits. Sure looks great, smells yummy, and feels firm and fine.

"It's-s-s really good s-s-stuff," the tempter hisses.

She takes a bite.

"Sure is! This is great! I feel great! Everything looks so. . . so different, so new and exciting. If this is death, I sure am enjoying it! Adam!" she shouts as she runs off stage right. The snaky creature slithers off stage left with a big grin on its face.

"It's so good, just super," Eve bubbles as they come on at stage right. "You have to try it!"

"But," Adam starts.

"No 'buts,' " she says. "It's great!"

"Well, you sure look fine to me after having some. Can't hurt." After taking a bite, he exclaims, "Wow, this is good! Why didn't God want us to have any?"

"Because He didn't want us to be wise like Him," she said. "He was jealous enough as it was."

"I'm feeling sleepy," Adam says. "We still have a little time on our break. Why don't we, uh, snuggle down here for a few minutes?"

They curl up together in front of the tree in the middle of the stage.

Adam sits up suddenly. "We're late. We better get back to work or God will be angry with us. Eve, come on, let's go."

"You smell! How long since you took a bath?" Eve asks.

"Why are you so critical all of a sudden?"

"I just noticed, that's all. You don't have to be so touchy!"

"Who's touchy? It was your tone of voice that started this whole ruckus!"

Eve begins to cry. "All I said was...."

"I think we better put something over us," Adam interrupts.

They walk over to the fig tree, pull off some larger leaves, tack them together with spikes from a thorn apple tree, and, feeling a little better, show off in front of each other in their new clothes.

"Hey, that looks pretty good on you. Now you don't look so hippy," Adam says.

Eve sinks to the stage and becomes very depressed. Adam leaves stage right to go get something to drink.

The curtain falls as we close our eyes and bow our heads.

Act three, the curtain and our eyes open as we raise our heads. We have before us the garden's center. But no one is around. Even the animals don't want to be there. Adam and Eve have been real grouches since they got back with their pin-spliced suits.

God comes on from stage left, looking for his friends. And they are nowhere in sight.

"Adam! Eve! Where are you?" He calls out.

He hears a rustle among the bushes stage right. Adam's head slowly rises above the shrubbery.

"Uh, we're over here, God. We, uh, didn't think you'd, uh, appreciate seeing us naked so we, uh, we, well, we made ourselves some clothes."

Warming up to his excuse, Adam stands up where God can see him. Eve's head peeps up over a nearby bush, looking from God to Adam and back.

"Not exactly designer fabrics and colors, but they will do," God says sadly. "You did it, didn't you?"

"What are you talking about? Oh, the tree? I wouldn't have even considered it if the companion YOU made for me hadn't dragged me to the tree over there and made me try it."

God stands there, stunned.

"Eve, what about it?" God says, turning to where she is still mostly hidden.

"That snake that lives over there tricked me into it. That's the honest truth. I wouldn't have done it otherwise. You know me, God, I wouldn't...."

"Eve, that's enough," God replies.

The whole stage is deathly quiet as Eve and Adam, separated by their respective bushes, stare at God. His head is bowed. Tears come down His cheeks.

"You have lost your appreciation for each other, for the plants and animals, and for Me. You blame someone else for your mistake. You lie." God stands there in a deep, sad silence now.

Then He speaks again. "From now on, you will be afraid of snakes and treat them as enemies. Eve, you will resent child-bearing, but you won't be able to get along without your man. Adam, the work you have enjoyed doing will become a drudgery to you. Gladly you have worked hard up to now, but from henceforth you will see it as a curse. You would have returned to the soil, but now you will be upset by that and will try to prevent it with pyramids, concrete vaults, and steel caskets. But you are still dust."

In their separate places on the stage, they all bow their heads, and they all weep.

The curtain descends.

The curtains reopens. Act four. It is the next morning. The three are standing outside a gate to the garden. It is newly constructed, and taller than they are. Adam and Eve have on fur and leather garments that are far more adequate and comfortable-looking than the leafy things they had on in Act three.

Adam breaks the long silence. "What is going to happen here?"

"Nothing," God replies. "Even if you come back, it will still look like work to you. You'll find something to complain about, someone to blame when things go wrong. That's as good as having guards with flaming swords."

"What about the tree of life? Won't that tempt people to come back some day?" Eve asks.

"They'll think so," God replies. "But when they get there, they will see the suffering it takes to get life from that tree. Some day, My Son will reach the tree of life and everyone will have a chance to know the pain and the agony it takes to live, to put aside the lies, blamings, complaints, the judgmentalism which puts everyone down who is different."

"What about us?" they ask.

"Those clothes I made for you will protect you from the harsher elements in the environment ... and from your own embarrassment. You've learned how to take care of plants and animals here. Just keep it up. Do your best. The world I've given you is a good world."

"Will you be around?"

"Yes, but you probably won't notice. When you are thankful, when you appreciate what you've got, when you share kindness and forgiveness and understanding and love, I'll be there and even then ... well, I'll be there," God concludes.

"Let's go," Adam says, turning his back toward God as God is about to reach out to hug him.

As they go off stage right, we hear Eve say, "God did a better job on your outfit than He did on mine. I look like a mess!"

"Aw, Eve!" Adam sighs loudly as the final curtain goes down.

Comment: The story of Cain and Abel tapped into experiences I had had with the criminal justice system in years past, and I set it into a rural Wisconsin county. I told it as a short story, but as I look at it now, I see it as something that could be readily dramatized with the help of individuals and with the help of the whole congregation at one point.

The narrator can be an older person. Cain and Abel should be young adult men. The pastor can be him/herself as can some of the other participants such as the council chairperson.

Cain's Sentence
Genesis 4:1-16

Narrator *(from pulpit)*: After the Gardeners, Adam and Eve, found a piece of good land to farm, they settled down and did fairly well for themselves. Except for the snakes, they got along with the animals. And, just as God had said, Eve wanted Adam and, by him, went through the dreaded childbirths for two sons. A third son, Seth, was born many years later.

The first boy they named Cain. Cain learned quickly how to farm. He helped his father Adam in the grain fields and became very expert in corn, alfalfa, and beans.

Cain *(from his place in the pew)*: I love the green of the plants.

Narrator: The other son, Abel, also learned quickly. Only he took interest in the dairy herds, and soon he handled that whole operation for the Gardeners.

Abel *(from his place in the pew)*: I love the calves and the milking.

Narrator: Good thing he did. He was up early every morning and in the barns every night to be sure the cows were milked. Even on Sundays!

All the Gardeners did well. The farm prospered. It was the largest spread in the county and no matter what the market conditions, one or another of their diversified program brought good prices.

They were good about going to church every Sunday. Fortunately, the services were late enough in the morning so that Abel had time to clean up and go along, and sit with his parents and his older brother. Things were going well.

Pastor *(from the front of the church)*: Let me call the administrative council chairperson forward for a special meeting of the council this morning. Everyone can stay for this. It won't take long and you can all have a say in the matter if you wish. Lennie, will you take over?

Ad. Council Chair *(coming to the front of the church from his/her pew)*: Thank you, Reverend. I am reminded of a story. Reverend was at home when his daughter had one of her little friends in. As he left the room to go to the kitchen, the little friend asked his daughter, "Does your house have a den?" "No," his daughter answered. "My dad growls like that all over the house!" Only kidding, Reverend.

Now, down to our business at hand. The Gardener boys each want to give a gift to the church. They have each had a good year and, in line with our policy of evaluating gifts before accepting them, I offer them this chance to make their presentations, after which we will vote on each. Cain, tell us what you have to offer.

Cain *(coming from his pew to stand next to the Chair)*: God has blessed me with a green thumb. Everything I plant grows and produces. Because of God's kindness, I want to give the church a complete repainting job on the inside as my gift. I have chosen a rich, dark green, my favorite color, for the sanctuary.

Chair: Any questions? You all understand what Cain wants to do? Good. Abel, what is your proposal?

Abel *(he comes up and joins Cain and Chair at the front)*: I have also had a good year this year and, just as God has blessed my good brother Cain with the gift of growing things, God has blessed me with a natural ability with animals. From the milk money I earned this past year, I want to buy something that we need pretty bad as a church, some decent folding tables for our church suppers, and a storage cart for them.

Chair *(with the boys still next to him/her)*: These boys have both offered generous gifts. I want to be sure you understand we can accept both. We don't have to choose between them. We can have them both. Got it? Okay. Any questions? Are you ready to vote?

All in favor of Cain's offer to paint the sanctuary a dark green, raise your hands. *(Hopefully the congregation will not raise their hands.)*

I know no one likes to turn down a gift, but it looks like Cain's offer is not accepted.

All in favor of the new tables and storage cart from Abel raise your hands. *(Hopefully enough do raise their hands. Even if none do, the Chair pretends they do.)*

Abel, on behalf of the congregation, I rule we accept your offer. Thank you very much. *(Chair turns to Abel and shakes his hand.)*

Cain, *(Chair turns to Cain, who walks up the aisle and out of the worship room)* we thank you for your offer but … *(he/she turns to the pastor)*

Pastor *(stands and comes to Chair)*: I'll call him when he gets home. I think we can adjourn the meeting.

(Abel and Chair sit down in their pews. Cain re-enters worship room and stands at the back with a phone in his hand.)

Pastor *(from front of worship room, not pulpit, with a phone)*: Cain, how are you doing?

Cain *(from the back on his phone)*: Fine. No problem. What do you want?

Pastor: You looked awfully angry when you left church this morning. You understood what happened, didn't you?

Cain: *(angrily)* I understood all right!

Pastor: No one doubted your desire to give something nice to the church. But you know what white elephants the church has been stuck with in the past by people whose gifts weren't evaluated first. That painting of Jesus in the Garden just doesn't go anywhere in the whole church and still look good.

Cain: Look, I don't want to talk about it, okay? I got work to do.

Pastor: You sound pretty angry. If that's so, it'll eat you alive. Anger is very dangerous. You stop thinking straight and may end up doing something you'll regret.

Look, the church isn't against you. The sanctuary does need painting. You got that much to the good. But the green would make it too dark in the church and the folks wish you'd have given them some choice in the color. Cain, are you listening to me?

Cain: I'm listening, Reverend.

Pastor: You still sound upset. Pull yourself together. Don't let the anger control you. We need you. Come on in tomorrow after you have a chance to think about it and let's talk about a better alternative gift. All right?

Cain: I'll think about it.

Pastor: Are you okay?

Cain: Fine, thanks. Yes, I'll see you tomorrow.

(Both put down their phones and sit down.)

Narrator: The pastor was worried about Cain. The young man was angry, but he sounded like other things were working on him as well. Disappointment that his gift wasn't acceptable to the church, guilt that he didn't present his gift very well, jealousy that his younger brother's gift was accepted by the church, those are powerful emotions mixed all together. But the Gardeners were a solid family, upstanding in the community. They'd work it out, he thought.

That evening, the pastor got a call from the chairperson of the Trustees.

Trustees Chair *(on phone, standing at his/her place in the pew)*: Reverend, I think we got a problem. I tried to call Abel to work out the details on his gift. I got Cain on the phone and I couldn't get him to put Abel on. He didn't sound right to me.

Pastor *(on the phone with the Trustee Chair)*: Thanks for calling. I'll get on it right away.

(Cain stands at back of worship room, with phone.)

Cain? Can you put Abel on? I need to talk to him.

Cain: Talk to me. What can I do for you?

Pastor: It's about Abel's gift. Where is he?

Cain: How should I know? Am I supposed to take care of my brother? He's a big boy now. He can take care of himself.

Pastor: Hey, easy does it. I just thought you'd know. By the way, how are the crops doing?

Cain: The weeds are bad. It took all week, including today, but I got rid of all of them. You kill weeds that mess up your farm.

Pastor: Where's Abel?

Cain: How should I know!? Lay off me. *(He hangs up and sits down.)*

(Pastor looks at phone and then sits down.)

29

Narrator: The pastor felt uneasy all night. He tossed and turned, knowing something was wrong, but not imagining just how bad things were. No pastor believes his people are capable of doing terrible things.

The next morning, it was on the news. Abel's body had been found out in the middle of one of Cain's corn fields. Cain had been arrested and was being held at the county jail. The pastor went right down without even having a cup of coffee.

(Cain walks down to the front and sits on the altar rail in front of the pulpit. The pastor comes up and sits next to him.)

Pastor: I came as quickly as I could. I heard about it on the radio just now. You don't have to say anything if you don't want to, but the state recognizes my right to hold conversations like this in confidence. I promise not to tell anyone anything you tell me.

Cain: I did it. I got Abel out in the field and I hit him. I was so jealous and angry I couldn't stand it. You were right. I didn't realize I had lost my head. When I saw Abel lying there so still, I screamed. And then I ran through the corn shocks and cut myself up some. Then it hit me what I had done. I went back, hoping he would be still alive, maybe even moving around okay. But he was just as I had left him. And he wasn't breathing.

Why did I have to hit him? He didn't do anything. He was a good kid. But when I saw him yesterday after church, all I could see was a smirky kid who had embarrassed me in front of the whole church. I hated his guts ... until I calmed down after I killed him. I was so messed up!

Pastor: Anger can do that to you. And that lets in jealousy, and pride, and the willingness to rationalize. Sounds like you let it all happen and get out of control.

Cain: What's going to happen to me?

Pastor: You'll be tried and probably convicted, and you'll go to prison for eight to ten years.

Cain: I'll lose the farm, won't I?

Pastor: Your folks are too old to run the whole operation with both you and Abel out of the picture. Seth is old enough to help with the dairy herd, but not in the fields yet. They will probably have to sell off the corn and hay fields.

Cain: I won't have any place to go when I get out of prison.

Pastor: You could come back to town.

Cain: You're too new around here. You don't know that town. They don't know what the word forgiveness means. I might as well be dead.

Pastor: We don't have capital punishment in this state.

Cain: What is the use of not having a field to grow corn? I wouldn't be worth anything without my fields. Maybe I'll get lucky and someone will kill me in prison.

Pastor: They won't touch you. They go after the effeminate homos and the child abusers. You, they'll ignore. Besides, if someone does come after you, there are some guards who will love to have an excuse to bust heads. There are always a few who just hope for a riot. Here, wear this cross. They'll razz you, but no one will come after you.

Cain (*putting the cross around his neck hesitantly*): God punishes me by sentencing me to live.

Narrator: What kind of God is it that makes clothes for Adam and Eve when they disobey Him? What kind of God is it that protects murderers? What kind of God is it that offers us another day of life?

We expect to find the compassionate God and Father of Jesus Christ in the New Testament. We remember too well some of the terrible stories of a vengeful God from the Old Testament. But God surprises us and even in these early stories is the one who gives us life.

Even when we lose it, even when we mess it up, even when we give up on it, God still gives us life. No family is safe from the potential of awful tragedy, even the best-appearing ones. But God does not give up on any of us. That's pretty good news.

Comment: One of the difficulties of telling the Genesis stories is that they are a slushing together of variant religious traditions and stories of the Hebrew tribes. Some stories do not lend themselves to a singular telling. The story of Noah is an excellent example.

To open it up to the variations within it, I imagined a family reunion many years after the flood and after Noah's grandchildren had heard the stories a hundred times from their own families. At the reunion, the children finally have a chance to ask Grampa Noah all their questions about the flood.

This story was done originally with the pastor attempting various voicing. Since timing is what makes a script like this come alive, the pastor may be wise in doing it him/herself. But competent, lively church members would provide a better voicing if they can sustain the sense of timing for their squabbles and questions.

Grampa Noah And When The Flood Came
Genesis 6 - 9

Narrator: Those of you who read the four chapters of text for this Sunday's sermon probably found yourself struck by the telling and retelling of the story of Noah, with variations in what animals went into the ark and how long before the ark settled onto dry ground, among other differences.

Modern biblical scholars largely agree that what we have in these four chapters is the intermingling of several different variations of the same story.

After the Hebrew tribes moved into the Holy Land and settled down, the ones in the northern half of the country had less contact with those in the south. In addition, the priestly tribes had their reasons for telling the old stories their own way. Everyone started out with much the same story known to them in Egypt, but after generations of telling them in their own regions, the stories became a little different. In an effort to unite the various regional and tribal groups, the stories were set down side by side by scribes. In some cases, they were slushed together. In others, they were told as they were by one group, and then told again as known by another group.

Does that leave you confused? Good. You're normal!

It is hard for us to look at the Bible as written by many different people in many different times and places, and we don't always think in terms of these writers having political or social reasons for putting down what they did as well as religious reasons.

To illustrate this problem, let me ask you to imagine a family reunion. Old Noah is getting up there in years and the families, who are scattered to the four winds in the generations since the Flood, want the grandchildren to meet the patriarch, the grand old man, of their family.

Ellie is from the family that moved up north. For some reason, her folks referred to God in a general way, never calling God by name, but calling God "the Lords." If you check the Bible, the translators could not say that. So they used the word "Lord" or "Lord God." Everything in the Noah story was simpler; there were fewer of everything, the way Ellie heard the story.

Ellie's cousin, Josh, is from down south. There, God is referred to by name. The translators of our Bible just use the word "God." The southern tradition found reasons for everything, explaining why God did the flooding and why He stopped it.

A third cousin, Peter, is a "PK," a preacher's kid. The way he heard it, God responded to everything in terms of the traditional rituals and worship patterns. Noah had to have at least seven pairs of all the animals or he would not have had enough for all the sacrifices he had to perform.

If you accept our premise of these three variations on the story, you will be able to relax with how Old Grampa Noah responds to the children when they have a chance to talk to him. If you are uncomfortable with this approach, take out your Bibles and read the four chapters for yourself. We won't take long.

(Noah and the three children/young adults come forward and sit where they can be seen by all. It may mean moving the pulpit to one side.)

Josh: Grampa Noah, how come you built the ark in the first place? You did it out of faith, right?

Peter: You did it because God told you to do it, right? You had to do everything just perfect, right?

Noah: Slow down! It started out as a big religious project. I'm not sure where my heart was on it. But it seemed to me to be what God wanted.

Ellie: Why did the Lord want it? What did He say?

Noah: Oh, the people were violent. There were wars all over the place. People were beating their children and each other. People were beating up on their own bodies with overwork, with booze, with drugs. They were tearing up God's hills, spoiling God's air, and gouging God's seabeds.

Ellie: So He had you gather up a pair of every kind of animal.

Peter: Seven pairs of all the clean animals!

Josh: There wouldn't have been enough room!

Noah: Did I tell it that many different ways? Oh, my! God was acting awful strange. Not like Himself at all.

Ellie: The Lord was grieved that He had made people, that they were so wicked.

Josh: Except for you, Grampa Noah, God saw that everyone was corrupt. To clean up the violence, He decided to destroy everyone else.

Peter: God didn't care about anyone but you, right? He needed someone to give Him burnt offerings, right?

Noah: It was a long time ago, children. Let me think. I would say God was very disappointed in what was going on. He was more concerned about it than the people were.

Ellie: Where did all the water come from?

Josh: That's easy. You see, there is water above the sky, held up there by a dome that God made. And there's water under the earth. It was easy. God just opened the flood gates below and the windows in the dome.

Noah: All I remember is that it started to rain. We climbed into the ark with as many animals as we could gather and as much food for them and us as we could store up. In our dry area, heavy rains could not soak in. And the place flooded.

Ellie: It rained forty days, didn't it?

Josh: A hundred and fifty days!

Peter: A year and a day!

Noah: We lost all track of time. It seemed the same in the storm and it seemed the same in the calm when that finally came. It was just a very long time.

Ellie: Could you see your house?

Noah: No. The flood was terrible. The great waters covered everything. Nothing survived. My parents died, your great-grandparents, and their parents, and all my neighbors, and all the livestock on the farms. It was terrible. We were in shock for weeks.

Ellie: When the flood was over, did you go back and bury your folks?

Josh: Ellie!

Noah: It's okay, Josh. Ellie, God's water did that.

Josh: How did the animals on the ark get along?

Noah: They did well. In fact, there were more when we got off the ark than we had brought on.

Peter: That's when you built the altar, right? And made the burnt offerings for God.

Noah: You certainly are anxious about those burnt offerings!

Ellie: Is the Lord going to flood the earth again?

Josh: God knows it won't do any good. People are bad no matter what and the flooding wasn't worth the effort!

Noah: That's pretty cynical.

Peter: God liked the burnt offerings and then repented of what He had done.

Noah: Peter, Peter, Peter. God isn't that impressed with burnt offerings. He wants justice and righteousness and compassion to flood the earth! He realized that the great flood He had brought was as violent as the very people He judged as violent. He did not want to ever be as bad as they were.

Ellie: Did you ever talk to the Lord again?

Josh: My folks said God promised that while the earth remains, seed time and harvest, cold and heat, summer and winter, day and night, shall not cease.

Peter: But only if we continue to bring offerings to God.

Noah: God did an interesting thing. He not only promised regularity in nature without our having to make the burnt offerings, Peter. He set a rainbow in the clouds after each storm to remind Himself that He would never do a flood again.

Ellie: Does the Lord speak to people and open and close doors like He did with you during the flood?

Noah: He tried that and discovered people made just as many excuses not to do what He wants as they did when He wasn't in direct contact with them. I think He figures we should at least try to talk to each other and help each other.

Narrator: Whoever put the book of Genesis together had a deep respect for the different points of view represented in the different tellings of Noah's story. It was pluralism working itself out in an intriguing way. Despite the differences in the themes of the three basic variations, and the arguments each group could have with the others, lying beneath all three is the truth that God's great care for His creation will supersede His wrath toward our violent ways. The God of grace is with us.

Comment: Up to this time, I had tried to handle the story sermons myself. With the encouragement shown for my dramatic efforts of the earlier weeks that summer, I decided to try to involve the congregation in a more direct way.

That year, a large hotel in a major U. S. city had collapsed, killing scores and injuring hundreds. I saw the story in a periodical which, unfortunately, I did not keep. The first interview in the script, the woman's experience, comes from that. With a few bits remembered from that incident, and knowing the congregation had a teacher from the Medical College of Wisconsin, an accountant, a union member, and an engineer working for the telephone company, I put together the following text and literally handed the various pieces to the respective church members as they came in the door. The first time I did this sermon, I was both the narrator and the reporter. I did it three years later in the same church with nearly all the same people in their roles, only I separated the two I had done. With that exception, the text is unaltered.

Each "actor" received a sheet indicating the order in which the actors were to be interviewed and suggesting where they should sit to facilitate the interviews. The folks usually sat in those spots anyway!

The church had a small microphone on a long cord which allowed us to take it to nearly anywhere in the front half of the church. While the acoustics were pretty good at the front and the back for speaking without a mike, people in the middle were not heard very well without it.

The Babel Disaster — You Are There
Genesis 11:1-8

Introduction by the pastor:

We have been looking at the stories from the book of Genesis from a more dramatic point of view than usual. The fall of the Tower of Babel lends itself to a special treatment. Most of us are old enough to remember the radio and television series "You Are There." With the help of members of our church's drama group and a few others, I have prepared this sermon using that format.

Studio Announcer: Today, our journey takes us to the Middle East, to a vast stretch of level river-bottom land between the Tigris (*tie - griss*) and Euphrates (*you - frate - eez*) Rivers. To the north, fifty miles, is the modern city of Baghdad, Iraq. To the southeast, two hundred fifty miles, is the top of the Persian Gulf where much of the war between Iraq and Iran is being fought.

We are on this vast plain between the rivers at the site of the ancient city of Babylon. Nearly four thousand years ago, a great towering temple was built. Tragedy struck soon after it was completed.

July 25th, in the eighth year of King Hammurabi (*ham - moor - rob - bee*) of Babylon, 1720 B.C., the collapse of the Temple of Etemenanke (*etta - men - non - key*), the fall of the Tower of Babel, YOU ARE THERE.

We take you now to our field announcer, who is at one of the rescue stations in the city of Babylon, barely a dozen yards from the fallen structure.

Field Announcer (FA): As I rode in this morning across the vast plain, the sky over the city was full of a gray, dark dust. The wind came up as I approached and has blown away a good deal of that ominous cloud. The sun shines now, but the scene of devastation before me is made all the more awful. The rubble rises dozens of feet, several stories into the air. There is a smell of tar and of death.

40

Oxen and camels are being used to move the rubble in search of victims. People are digging with sticks, boards, anything they can find. There are tents and shanties erected near the rubble, probably for people looking for family members who may still be in the ruins.

I am at an aid station next to the fallen tower. There is a woman here, her arm in a sling. Ma'am, can you tell me and our listeners what happened?

Woman: It was a very hot day. The odor of the tar between the bricks was very strong. A lot of people had come to the temple. A nice party was being held in honor of the building committee and trustees. We were in the great hall on the ground floor. We heard a great crash outside. It was worse than thunder. The floor shook.

Then ... then ... the walls seemed to turn. It was very strange. Then dust began to fall, and bricks, and beams, and arches crashed down everywhere.

Then silence, and dust. I hadn't had a chance to move. I felt my right arm hurting very much. I couldn't feel my legs at the time. It was dark. And so quiet.

Then I heard a voice. It was my little son. He had been standing next to me when everything began to fall. I realized I still had hold of his hand with my left hand.

"Mom, are we alive?" he asked.

I nearly cried. "Yes," I said, choking on my tears and the dust. "Can you move?" I asked him. He told me he couldn't move anything but his head. "Squeeze my hand," I told him. He did, and I knew he wasn't hurt too bad.

We lay there in the dark, wondering if anyone would know where to look for us. We wondered what had happened to Dad and Sis. They had left to find the food table and we were looking for a place to sit ... when ... I'm sorry.

"Will they ever find us? Will they ever get us out?" my son asked. He was about to panic. I felt like I was, too. But I tried to stay calm. "Yes," I told him, "they'll come. God will protect us."

"No, He won't," my son said. "A street preacher said God would destroy this temple."

41

I tried to reassure him that God didn't do those kinds of things. And I tried to get him to sing a song with me about God being so good. We sang it over and over. I don't know how we would have stayed alive if we hadn't had our faith.

Apparently we were near the entrance. I felt something touch my leg. Rescue workers had begun digging at the main gate and we were among the first found. The entrance arch had fallen toward us and held together enough to protect us from other debris.

They've been digging for days, but they ... they ... still haven't found ... There I go again.

FA: What can we learn from this?

Woman: Grasping the hand of God. If everyone would walk with God, instead of squabbling, things would be better.

(Mayor, who sits at the back, strides up to announcer as he finishes his interview with the woman.)

FA: The gentleman approaching me appears to have much authority in this city, from the way he is dressed and the way he walks. I gather, sir, that you are the mayor. What is your reaction?

Mayor: Well, our lovely city has many great features. We are very proud of our city. We like it here. Our city is number one!

This tragedy has been a terrible one. But we will rebuild. We are a great city. Everyone knew it before and they will know it again. Our city is number one.

When the religious community first approached us with their idea about a skyscraper temple, we thought it was a great idea. It would make people notice our city. The building could be seen for over twenty miles in every direction here on the plain. It would mean jobs for thousands of workers. We had to tear down two hotels where old people lived and we condemned buildings where there were a number of businesses in order to do it. Those old people and small businessmen gave up their homes and businesses so that we could be number one.

This has been a terrible tragedy. But we like it here. We will rebuild. Our city is number one.

FA: Is there any lesson this tragedy teaches us?

Mayor: What? Oh, nothing.

42

(Mayor returns to his seat as announcer goes over to "Federal Inspector" [FI] who is seated on the aisle.)

FA: This gentleman's badge indicates he is a federal inspector. What has the National Safety Board done about this?

FI: Well, we have impounded all the structural members in warehouses as we have dismantled them. The rescue crews have cleared rubble away as they have gone along and the heavy equipment teams have then removed the arches and pillars for our perusal.

It appears that by hyper-thermal action, the binding material between the bricks lost its cohesion, thus becoming increasingly subject to structural stress of the superstructure. But we will have to examine all of the remnants of the temple before we can bring a judgment of blame.

What seems to have slowed down the rescue efforts is that people don't seem to understand what each other is saying.

FA: Any observations you'd like to make, Mr. Inspector?

FI: These people are as fragmented as their building. Something will need to bind them together.

(Announcer moves from federal inspector to the doctor who is also on the aisle near him.)

FA: Near me now is a man who appears to be a medical person, a doctor. Can you tell us how the rescue operation has proceeded?

Doctor: Everything has gone far more slowly than we thought it would. No one imagined that our technology would fail. Everyone was so sure the temple could stand forever. Our scientists and engineers reassured us. With a temple so great, we felt secure that God wouldn't let anything happen to us.

But it did. There must have been a thousand people in the temple when it collapsed. Hot as it was outside, the high ceiling of the first level had a cooling effect. If the building had stood a little longer, there would have been ten thousand in there.

I was on my way to the party. You could see the building for miles, towering over everything. It was magnificent. I heard a rumbling. As I watched the temple, the topmost section began to turn. Then I realized the whole building was beginning to twist and fall in on itself. I just ran. I knew there were people inside and I could see this was the worst disaster ever to happen in our city.

So far we have found 380 dead. There are about a hundred who somehow survived. It has been about five days and they are finding fifty to a hundred bodies each day. The work is far from over.

I must return to the aid station. Many of the survivors are still in need of care.

FA: In light of this tragedy, what needs to happen here?

Doctor: A whole new spirit is needed.

FA: I have with me a man who appears to be a mason, a bricklayer. Were you a part of the construction crew?

Mason: What a mess, hey? Me an' the boys been bettin' how come dat bugger fell. Dey never let none of us in to the party 'cuz we wasn't good enough for 'em. We was good enough ta lay dere bricks, but not good enough to go ta da bash or even ta see da finished product.

Them super-religious guys, not the pastor, but them building committee types or whatever you call them, dey wouldn't let none of us touch the finish work on the top temple. Dey says it was God's house and we was too dirty to work on it.

More power to 'em, we says. But dey got our goat. I hope dey was inside when that bugger went crash.

Dey was so snooty to us when we tried to tell 'em about the bricks. We says dem bricks wouldn't hold no weight. They wasn't tough enough. Half of 'em broke in our hands. But the contractor said they was what we had to use, and da building committee wanted everything done by the deadline.

So we went on strike. We didn't want none of our guys hurt by them walls come tumblin' down. Finally, after four weeks, dey come to us and says they was making the bricks different, with straw or something. When we tried 'em, dey was tougher so we went back to work.

Hey, the temple went up quick after we got them new bricks. No more waste.

But did anyone thank us for it? No way. They thanked each other. What bums! Serves 'em right the thing crashed.

FA: Anything more you want to say?

Mason: People gotta respect each other. We need a whole new spirit around here.

(Announcer goes across the aisle to accountant.)

FA: I am at the office of an accounting firm. You were involved with the project, I gather. Were you in the temple?

Accountant: I didn't plan to attend the party. I was invited, but, well, there were so many misunderstandings and downright rip-offs that I got sick of the whole project long before it was finished.

For one thing, I was disturbed by the way subcontractors got their bids. One group was headed by the ma ... a prominent man's son. I saw the bids and that one was not the lowest. Another subcontractor got paid every week, but I never received any time cards or invoices for materials from them. When I asked my boss about it, he said to keep my nose out of it. People always do business that way and you can't change the world, he said. It made me sick.

For another, the strike was a big hoax. Even though we have had high unemployment around here, those guys wanted more money. They talked about bricks, but when they got their higher pay, they went back to work. We still got bricks from the same company after the strike as we did before the strike.

For another, they changed the bookkeeping system halfway through. As I figure it, someone skimmed off about two hundred thousand.

When the temple collapsed, I almost wish I'd been there. I should have said something a long time ago. But I was afraid of losing my job. What would you have done?

FA: Do you have any further observation you would like to make?

Accountant: The pride, the greed, the egos. They all have to change. We need a whole new spirit around here.

FA: I am told by our producer that the general contractor is now available to speak with us. Perhaps you can tell us how the temple collapsed.

Contractor: I really can't say what happened. We had the finest quality materials. The craftsmanship was topnotch. The architects have been eminently capable. The supervision was excellent. We are very proud of our achievement.

This has to be an act of God. There must have been an earthquake. Perhaps there was a fault undiscovered in the ground.

The temple was 297 feet high. It covered four city blocks. The first level was 150 feet high. In this hot climate, the high ceiling would provide a real cooling effect. There were six temples, each 20 to 30 feet high, placed on top of each other, the upper ones being smaller than the lower ones. The building looked like it was terraced. Because of the great height of the first level, we constructed two external stairways, one up along the wall to the top of the first level. Interior stairs sufficed for the upper temples. The second stairway we built approached the east wall perpendicularly. It was over 220 feet long, rising the 150 feet to the top of the first temple.

We used that second staircase as a structural member to anchor the east wall. It was built massively so that it could assure a load-bearing role in the architecture. Because it was such a strong buttress, we built the rest of the temple to lean on it.

Several witnesses told me it was the east staircase that was the first thing to go.

I can't understand it.

Maybe the bricklayers sabotaged it. They complained about the heat, the wages, the bricks, everything. They thought they were so high and mighty that they even asked to do the finish work in the sanctuary of sanctuaries. I thought they'd go on strike about that, too. But that was the last task. I think they went on the first strike so they could get a vacation. With nothing to do after the rough work they did on the top, they had nothing to gain.

I'm to work with the federal inspectors to determine what happened. When we discover who to blame, we can make certain it won't happen again.

FA: What do you think will happen now?

Contractor: When we find out who to blame, that will take care of everything.

FA: Our last interview has been lined up with the pastor of this great temple. You were the driving force behind this tower, weren't you?

Pastor: Our dream was a good dream. We have always known that people will give to build a building before they will give to help in mission projects. Heaven knows there are enough needy people living on the Shinar plain. But to bring God into more people's lives, to impress them that God is present among us, we envisioned a great temple that would dominate the landscape, one no one could ignore.

When some engineers in our congregation reported a new construction process of using tar to bind the bricks together, we felt we had the necessary technology to construct our dream temple. We sold our dream over the media and people sent us money from all over the plain. Everyone wanted to be proud of the new temple. When we promised to write each donor's name on the bricks they were willing to buy, the money really poured in, even from people who had no religion. We had enough money to underwrite the costs within a year.

Construction began. But so did the problems. The temple became a political football. The mayoral candidates fell all over each other trying to get on the bandwagon. It became a contractor's boondoggle. Everyone tried to make money off of us. It became our labor negotiator's nightmare trying to work things out with the labor unions. It became a theoretical disaster. Everyone had a theory about how best to get the height, about how best to buttress the walls, how to let light in, what themes were most appropriate to decorate each temple level (there were seven!). I could not believe the confusion. Each specialist was using his own jargon. Each church leader seemed to get his ego so involved in supporting his own ideas that he didn't listen to what anyone else was saying. It was awful. I still don't know how the temple was ever completed.

Wonder of wonders, it was finished. Late, but nonetheless finished. And it did dominate the plain. I waited for people to come and praise God, to report how they could no longer ignore God, to offer themselves to serve the needy through the temple.

But the only ones who came were the old standbys. Oh, a lot of people came to see their bricks. They complained when they couldn't find them or because theirs weren't in a prominent position.

How can people be so confused about what we were doing? God must have hardened their hearts. I don't know.

And then for this awful thing, I've had a mass funeral every day since the temple fell. I'm told it'll be weeks before all the dead have been found.

Excuse me, I need to meet with some of our laypeople. They have been visiting the families of the dead to bring comfort and help. They need help keeping their sanity. May God help me keep mine!

FA: What lesson is there in this great tragedy?

Pastor: Maybe what we need is for God to come down here Himself, to meet with us, give us some advice on how to live together, warn us about how dangerous bad motives are, maybe give us a new spirit so we will understand each other and care about each other better. That will be the new birth of religion.

FA: Thank you, Pastor.

This has been a great tragedy. Despite the winds, there is still dust enough to darken this city early in the evening. The tar smell remains strong in the air and the grim smell of crushed flesh still hovers over the ruins here.

Who is to blame? Is it man, his ego, his carelessness, his greed?

Is it God, bringing judgment, or just a natural calamity?

What can be done? All spoke one language, but they used different vocabularies that made it hard for them to understand each other. They each saw things from their own point of view and could not see beyond that.

Several felt the coming of a new spirit, a holy spirit, could resolve this.

But there are two questions: Who will send it? And who will live by it?

And now back to the studio.

Studio Announcer: In that catastrophe, in which hundreds of lives were lost, humankind experienced for the first time the problems of communication failure. Each segment of the population was so wrapped up in itself that no one knew what the others were saying. The call for a new spirit was to be fulfilled at Pentecost in 29 A.D. when the Christian Church was born in the upper room.

48

The followers of Jesus were understood by people of every known language.

If that spirit had been known and shared 1750 years earlier, there would not have been the disaster on July 25th, 1720 B.C., the collapse of the temple of Etemenanke (*etta - men - non - key*), the fall of the Tower of Babel. YOU ARE THERE.

Comment: One of the great figures of Genesis, Abraham, amazed me the first time I read the story of his argument with God over His plan to destroy Sodom. With that in mind, I got to wondering how Abraham might have handled his anxiety over how his obedience to God was paying off. I chose a time early in his career when that anxiety would have been high.

The first time I did this story sermon, a friend let me use a classic old black telephone that dated from the early '40s. With it, I conducted a one-sided conversation with God, much on the order of Bob Newhart's technique, that is, repeating much of what God had said.

This time, I did the same thing, but wished I had the technology to handle the conversation like Bill Cosby had in his "Noah" skit, having a tape recording for the voice of God.

Since starting to work on this book, I realized a lay person on a microphone out in the open or down behind the pulpit, or even at the back of the church, could do the God-voice.

For this text, I will write God's part in CAPS and then write underneath in parentheses how the pastor could phrase his response in the Bob Newhart style.

I leave the reader to imagine which would work best.

I Want To Go South, Lord
Genesis 12:1-10

Commentator (Pastor or lay person): We've been going through the stories of Genesis this summer. So far, we have seen God, using the tool of love, fashion a creation out of the raw material of the crashing waters of chaos. Despite the mess-up of Adam and Eve, God still clothed them. Despite Cain's murder of Abel, God sentenced Cain to a life protected by God. Despite humankind's wickedness, God promised Noah there never again would be a flood to try to eradicate evil. Why use evil to get rid of evil?

Are you amazed at how much grace God shared with those people? Christians think of grace as a New Testament matter. But that isn't so. German Christian theologians have used the word *Heilsgeschichte* ("holy history") to point to the fact that God has *always* been in the business of forgiving us and finding ways to work within our limitations to forge a life of blessing for all creation.

Before examining those stories, we probably thought that those people had an easier time obeying God because God was able to speak to them directly. After watching Adam and Eve squabble and fall away from God, after agonizing over Cain's murderous act, we begin to know better. Let me further illustrate how God's graceful involvement with us is not easier just because we could have direct access. It was not easier for Abraham.

In these verses of chapter 12, Abraham, known in those days as Abram, accepts God's promise of making of him a great nation, of giving him a land, and of making of him a blessing to the nations. He leaves behind the great commercial city of Ur of the Chaldees and heads over to the new property. God sends him through it, from north to south, occasionally reminding him about the promise.

In the south, the Negeb Desert area, Abram does not like what he sees. The earlier part of the trip was not that fantastic either.

52

Now he faces wall-to-wall wastelands, horizon-to-horizon famine. Word comes to him that further south there is a better place, Egypt, with its great Nile River and rich delta region where turnips and figs grow as big as watermelons.

He decides it is time to check in with God and see if he can keep going to get out of this awful place. He keys in (*dials*) God's number, 1-800-555-0001.

Abram: Hello, God? This is Abram. Uh, I want to go south, Lord.

God: WHAT'S THE PROBLEM?

(What is the problem?)

Abram: Do you realize how hot it is down here? It's terrible. There's no food. All you can see is sand everywhere. We can't stay here and going back north does not seem like a good idea to me.

God: WHAT DO YOU EXPECT! THAT'S A DESERT. YOU WENT TOO FAR.

(What do I expect? [*pause*] Oh, it's a desert. [*pause*] You say I went too far?)

Abram: Well, I'd really like to go to this Egypt.

God: BUT IT'S HOTTER THERE.

(It's hotter, you say.)

Abram: More heat I sure don't need!

God: WHAT'S YOUR REAL PROBLEM?

(You don't think the heat and famine are my real problem?)

Abram: God, I guess I'm just worn out. I've been trudging through this place for weeks now. I was all full of hope when I left Ur. And I was excited to see a new country. And there were some pretty places back up north. When I got to Shechem and to that place near Bethel, I was proud of being your servant and coming here. Those were real high moments for me. But look at all the good it did. I had no impact on the people who lived there. They haven't changed since I built those shrines. The people are all the same, no sense of commitment, no sense of hope. Only the same old ways of doing things. I went right through them. No blessing, no nothing! Nothing's changed. I just want to get on. I want to go south.

God: NOTHING HAPPENED! DO YOU REALIZE NO ONE WAS HARMED?

(Nothing happened? No one was harmed, you say.)

Abram: I hadn't thought of it that way. After all, the people who live there now got it by using terrorism and that made refugees and they are now using terrorist tactics to try to get it back. And the army is as vicious as it wants to be in response. It's a mess. No wonder you want to give it to a third party. But why me? I just want to go south, Lord.

God: SO WHAT ELSE IS WRONG?

(Why do I think something else is wrong?)

Abram: It's a relief to know we got through safely but I'm still worn out.

God: WHY ARE YOU STILL TIRED?

(Why am I still tired?)

Abram: Why am I still tired! You know who came along with me! They are wearing me out! They are so petty, always fussing about something or other, they're picky, they have to have their own way about everything. I'm sick of it!

God: HOW MANY ARE WEARING YOU OUT?

(How many what? Oh.)

Abram: How many …?

God: YES, HOW MANY?

(How many …?)

Abram: Lot's wife really gets me. He's the salt of the earth, but she, she's a real blockhead. She's always on me about going back, that we can't try this or that, that we shouldn't try anything new. God, she has to control everything. Harassing! That woman is on me all the time! She's going to look back one too many times!

God: MAYBE SHE'S AFRAID … LIKE YOU.

(She's afraid? You've got to be kidding. What? Like me?)

Abram: She's … I'm not … How did you know? I'm getting old. I feel so drab, so frumpy and lumpy. My friends all have nice houses and better stuff. Most of them don't speak to me and those that do always find ways to make me feel like I haven't done anything with myself compared to them. And I find it easy to agree with them!

God: YOU'RE NOT A BLESSING.

(Right. I'm not a blessing.)

Abram: But I have tried, Lord. I try to be helpful, forgiving, understanding, fair, forthright. I defend my friends, speak up for what is right.

God: AND ALL YOU GET IS FLACK.

(Flack is right!)

Abram: Lots of flack. It's scary.

God: HOW BAD?

(Well, awful scary.)

Abram: It seems like every time I turn around, Lot's wife gets to me.

God: ANYONE ELSE?

(Anyone else?)

Abram: Uh, well, there's uh … Hmmmm. Sara's been a peach. Lot has been great. The servants have been pretty good, I guess. You know, I got so wound up I stopped being thankful for the folks who are doing fine and working well with me. I've been through this cycle before, realizing what I have to be thankful for and getting over a lot of the pain and confusion. But then I stop and I get mad again and get upset and scared all over again.

God: YOU'LL GET OVER IT.

(I hope I'll get over it!)

Abram: You'd think I'd learn by now.

God: ANYONE ELSE? ANYTHING ELSE BOTHERING YOU?

(No, no one else. But now that you mention it …)

Abram: Yes, something else is bothering me. Your promises. You promised a son. Here we are in our late seventies and no son. No son to inherit the land You are giving me. Are You ever going to come through for me?

God: YOU SEEM TO WANT EVERYTHING RIGHT NOW.

(Yes, I do want everything right now.)

Abram: Lord, I left a perfectly good life at Ur. I didn't complain. I've done all you asked. But there's no son.

God: I'M WORKING ON IT.

(You're working on it.)

Abram: Big deal! You're working on it.

God: YOU HAVE TO GIVE ME TIME.

(Give you time!?)

Abram: How much time have I got to give you? I'm 75 now! I'm going south.

God: SO GO.

(So go?)

Abram: I should just go?

God: YES.

Abram: You're willing to let me go?

God: YES.

Abram: Don't you want me to stay?

God: YES, BUT I ALSO WANT YOU TO GO.

(You want me to stay and you want me to go.)

Abram: Why?

God: BECAUSE I WANT YOU TO MEET MORE NATIONS.

(Meet more nations?)

Abram: You really mean that. You want me to meet more nations. Is it okay if I go to Egypt for the rest of the year?

God: GO. GET REST. YOU'LL BE BACK.

(Get rest? I'll be back?)

Abram: You think I'll be back. I can't promise anything, especially without a son. Why come back without someone to inherit my land?

God: ONE THING AT A TIME.

(Okay, one thing at a time.)

Abram: I'll try to take it one day at a time. Maybe I can get to understand the Egyptians and maybe I can be a better blessing that way.

God: ANYTHING ELSE BOTHERING YOU?

(No, nothing else is bothering me.)

Abram: Yes, I'm still scared ... like Lot's wife and a lot of other folks I know. So stay with us, Lord.

Commentator: God's patient grace is there in this story of Abram. But faith isn't any easier nor does it come any more naturally just because you are closer to God. There are still times of fear, upset, anger, and doubt. That's why we need to meet together and why we tell the old, old stories.

And we have a chance to be reminded in other ways. Let's join Abram in heart and mind as we sing the hymn, "Guide Me, O Thou Great Jehovah."

> *Guide me, O Thou great Jehovah,*
> *Pilgrim through this barren land.*
> *I am weak, but Thou art mighty,*
> *Hold me with Thy powerful hand.*
> *Bread of heaven, Bread of heaven,*
> *Feed me till I want no more.*
> *Feed me till I want no more.*

Comment: To get an unusual angle on their story, storytellers sometimes take on the persona of someone in or close to the event they are describing.

The following look at the story of Abraham's sacrifice of his son Isaac comes from a neighbor who lived in that region, a practitioner of religion and life as it was understood by the indigenous inhabitants.

Dramatically, the pastor can read it out loud as if he were writing it, as I did. Or he can introduce it and let someone from the congregation read it.

On Sacrificing Others
Genesis 22:1-22

Commentator: Our character telling the story is one of the local landowners who has lived in northern Canaan all his life. He is a good son as well, as you will hear in a moment, for he tells the story of Abraham and Isaac to his father.

But even this non-Hebrew cannot tell the story without God being the central character. What is God like?

Reader:

Dear Father,

You've asked me to keep an eye on Abraham, the great prince whose people sojourn among us. Well, he hasn't caused any trouble lately, either. I told you about when he first moved in from across the northern border, how he and some of our neighbors put together a war party to go rescue his nephew Lot from those outlaw kings. But he has been going about his business of raising sheep ever since. As hard as sheep are on grazing lands, he keeps them moving so they don't eat all the way down to the roots, and the forage returns very well by the time he completes the rotation.

Usually, we have problems with the kids of these foreigners. They say it's our kids that start the fights. But ours wouldn't do such a thing! As you know, Abraham never had a son until about seven years ago. Oh, he did have one boy by his wife's maid. But Sarah, his wife, sent the maid and the boy away right after Isaac was born. You could see the light go out of Abraham's eyes when they left. But you know Abraham. He gave them all he could and placed them in his God's hands.

Abraham has a strange God! I'd have sent Sarah away and kept the maid and both boys! But I digress.

All this is to say that we've had no trouble because of bickering children.

You asked me not only to report the obvious things about these foreigners. You want to know about their way of life, their religion, their special skills.

You've heard about most of that, how they wander from place to place with their sheep, how they set up shrines here and there depending on where Abraham has a talk with his God. Before I forget, did I tell you he frequently uses our holy places and adds his own altar there once in a while? I don't think he believes in our gods, but he told me once his God was also the God of all, including the Egyptians, the Amorites, the Jebusites, the Hittites, and even of us Canaanites. I've never heard those other foreigners mention that. They never heard of Abraham's "Most High" or "Everlasting God." Most of them think he's a little strange because of his beliefs.

But I have this to say for him. He keeps his word. Even when those outlaw kings went into negotiations with him, he was fair and he hasn't ever gone back on what he promised. If he weren't such a nice old man, I'd be nervous, because men of such integrity can be quite unyielding.

Again, forgive my digression. I write to tell you of something really strange that happened this past week.

Early Sunday morning, Abraham, his son Isaac who is about seven now, and two young men from his camp stopped here. Abraham asked me to look in on Sarah while he was gone. She hasn't been feeling too well lately. He has plenty of people in his camp to see to her needs, but he wanted to be sure that if anything went wrong, maybe some of us who have lived here all our lives would know of something that might help.

Then he told me this strange story about his strange God telling him to go and sacrifice Isaac. The light was out of his eyes again, just like when the maid's little boy left.

I had warned him. He should have sacrificed Isaac long ago. The Hebrews haven't learned that you have to sacrifice to your god before you get too attached to the child. But Abraham had stuck to just sacrificing lambs. He didn't believe me when I warned him that even his God would demand his firstborn son as a gift of faith.

A man has to prove how faithful he is to his God and to his nation by being able to give up the life of his son.

We've talked about that a good deal over these past seven years but he kept saying that every child is precious in God's eyes. But even more important, his God had promised that Isaac's children would one day be a great nation. That strange idea kept him from knowing the truth. He was blind to the fact that no one child carries the hope of the future.

It is our faithfulness, not our children's, that is the key to the future.

He always laughed and asked if we'd be so willing to give up our fine homes and fast camels as easily as we gave up our firstborn sons. He has a strange sense of humor.

I guess because of our talks, he came here. He didn't say any more at the time. I really sympathized with him. Isaac is a bright boy and a hard worker already at his age. A few more years and Isaac would be strong enough to protect his father from enemies. Now Isaac was going to have to protect his father from his God, just like our firstborn have protected us from ours from the beginning.

Abraham had another problem. He had given up his whole past, his whole heritage, to come and live here among us. He has no relatives here. He has no burial place here. He just has the one well he negotiated for with Abimelech. He has no roots. He often told me that he put his roots into the future, the promise his God had made that Isaac would father a great multitude more numerous than the stars. You could see Abraham really glow when he spoke of that promise from his God. And now here was his God taking that future away from him by calling for the sacrifice of Isaac.

A man with no past, a future that was ending before it began, and a present that was unspeakable. I went to hold him and assure him of our being neighbors. As I did, I felt more like he was holding me. Maybe a man in his faithful obedience has more strength than he realizes in the midst of his tragedies.

Well, he came back today, after being gone a week. And there was Isaac! When he left, you could tell Abraham was going to go through with it. I'd have bet my fine house and my fastest camel on it, I was so sure.

You know what he told me? He said he almost did it. He'd even tied up the boy and put him on the sticks for the fire. He said his God stopped him. "You have not kept back anything from me," his God said. And his crazy God even had a ram stuck in the underbrush near the altar for Abraham to use instead!

I guess it goes to show the Hebrews have enough faith that they could sacrifice their sons like we do. But on the other hand, maybe their God doesn't want them to do it. To me that says we don't have to be afraid of the Hebrews.

If they can't let their kids do their dying for them, you can bet they aren't going to die for anything.

Just as he was leaving, Abraham said, "You are willing to lay down the life of others for you. But are you willing to lay down your life for others?" He seemed very serious when he said it.

I didn't quite know what to do with that. But I thought I'd better pass it on to you.

Your loving second son,
Ephron

Comment: A good story can be done a number of ways. A story about Jacob lent itself as a short story when I did it. Since then, I have come to see it as a radio drama, not unlike those frequently heard in the '40s and '50s in which the hero narrates and has some dialogue with a limited number of other characters. Sound effects would be nice and could be handled by a creative team working on this story.

Those who study the biblical story closely will realize I have taken some liberties, as most storytellers do. But I hope that in doing so, I have not detracted from how God and Jacob struggled that night on the bank of the River Jabbok. By the way, I understand some psychotherapists use the technique described here in certain circumstances. Integrating "modern" activities into ancient stories does not necessarily spoil either.

Jacob And The Night Wrestler
Genesis 32:22-32

Jacob: One never knows how God will strike you in a personal encounter. You can take that both ways in my case. We not only had a strong encounter, I came out of it with a bad limp! But I am way ahead of my story.

My name is Jacob. I travel with my two wives, two maids, eleven sons, many herdsmen, and my flocks. We are traveling back from Haran. Ahead a few days, I will be home. And my brother Esau will be waiting for me. He will probably have blood in his eyes. You see, I cheated him a little. Well, if you can say conniving with our mother so that our father Isaac gave me the family blessing and made me primary heir, even though Esau is older, is a little cheating. Actually, it was a big cheat. And Esau could never forgive me for that.

But I can't go back to Haran or my father-in-law will kill me! Funny how a cheater can fall for a cheat. When I first went to Haran, he promised me Rachel, his younger daughter, if I would work for him for seven years. So I did it and was married.

Leah: Jacob, dearest, it is morning. Time to wake up.

Jacob: Good morning, my love! I have waited so long for — what is this! You aren't Rachel! Leah, what are you doing here? I married Rachel last night at the feast!

Leah: Laban, my father, had me dress in heavy veils and wear one of Rachel's dresses. Please don't be angry. I love you as much as she does and I will be a good wife! Please don't put me out!

Jacob: That man! How could he deceive me like that? You are the one with bad eyes! How could I be so gullible?

Laban had me. I couldn't be cruel to Leah and I had to have Laban's blessing on the marriage in order to marry my real love.

But I was so crazy for Rachel that I let him talk me into another seven years of free labor with his flocks to marry Rachel.

It would have to be her. He only had the two girls!

I tried to get back at him by some creative genetics and ended up with the best flocks for myself. When he saw what I'd done, I decided I would be better off facing Esau than Laban! Just as we were leaving, Rachel came running out of her father's tent.

Rachel, what are you doing?

Rachel: Hurry! Don't waste any time. We have to leave right now!

Jacob: What's in that sack?

Rachel: My father's household gods!

Jacob: I took the bag from her, opened it up, and there inside were several pieces of religious statuary. The man would go wild when he discovered she had stolen them. Too late now. We were on our way and there would be no reconciling with him.

But now we are approaching Canaan. And I will have to deal with Esau. Maybe the quarter century that has passed since I left will have mellowed him. But maybe not. Just in case, I have split my family and flocks so that an attack would not destroy all of my holdings in one blow.

Leah and my sons by her are with the group several miles north. Rachel, Joseph, and I are together with the southern flocks.

We camped for the day here by the ford of the River Jabbok. Night is coming and it is finally cool enough to travel. I already sent several flocks ahead, along with a number of other gifts, as a peace offering to Esau. Would he take them and be more forgiving toward me? If not, I had no place else to go.

Bilhah, Rachel's maid, has taken Joseph across the river along with the flocks. Rachel is the last to leave.

Rachel: Jacob, darling, please come with me. Father is not too far behind and we will need all the extra time we can get to stay ahead of him.

Jacob: You go on. I'll stay and clean up the camp site so he won't see that we've been here. I'll be along in a little while.

Rachel: Jacob, you worry me. You've been so depressed lately. I wish you would come now and let the winds sweep away the signs of our being here.

Jacob: You must go. Someone has to take care of the baby Joseph. If your father comes, I don't want us both caught and killed by him. So go. I'll be along.

She looked long at me, then turned and went on across the river.

When she was over the hill on the other side, I went back to the fire. Its last coals were going out. I kicked some sand on them, and, instead of cleaning up as I said I would, I slumped down on a rock and mulled over what I faced.

Laban and his army are coming up behind us. Esau has an army of four hundred out there waiting for us. I really don't have a chance. I've cheated both of them. It's me they want. Maybe they'll leave my wives and sons alone if they don't find me. I can't hide out here anywhere. It's so desolate. They've both got good scouts and would track me down. It would solve everything if my body was found downstream in the river. No confrontation with either of my enemies. No more hassle between competing wives. No more noisy children to disrupt my every privacy. It would be so easy.

I started along the river bank, looking for stones I could put in my pockets to weigh me down. As I found a good-sized one, I rejoiced that I wouldn't have to worry about all the decisions necessary to settle my family and flocks, if Esau would let me in at all. With each rock I found, I felt another worry melt away. After a little while, I was actually feeling very free and very happy in my strange way, splashing along the river, ready to just let myself fall in and let the stones carry me to the bottom of the stream. Everyone would think I slipped and fell when I tried to ford, or that I was caught in a flash flood. But I'd be free!

God: Hey, idiot, I've got a stone for you!

Jacob: Watch what you're doing. That almost hit me.

God: Better duck, dummy, because here comes another one. You want to drown yourself, you're going to need more rocks than that.

Jacob: Where the stranger came from I don't know but he began pelting me with all kinds of rocks and stones. And was calling me names and belittling me in every way he could.

God: You are one lousy excuse for a man. *(Makes grunting noises intermittently as he throws)* You can't take any heat. Here you are, ready to chicken out on the future, leave your kids in the hands of relatives. Some blessing you are.

Jacob: I didn't have a lot of time to think. But at first, I knew he was right, but then, with his constant peppering me with small stones along with his insults, I began to get angry.

You don't have to rub it in.

God: You've got no guts. You are scared to face anything. You could have grabbed Rachel when she came running out with Laban's gods and taken her and them back to him, but no, you had to run.

Jacob: This guy was in my face. He wouldn't stop.

God: You keep asking God to keep His promises and you haven't kept yours. What a mess you are!

Jacob: I turned my back and started to walk away. One of the stones he threw hit me hard just above the hip. I went down in agony, pain leaping through my right leg from where the stone hit, all the way to my toes. With rage, I grabbed at the stranger from the ground, caught his leg and pulled him down. He came down on top of me hard. I was so furious I lashed into him with everything I had.

The stranger kept up his insults and I tried to shut him up any way I could. But he was so strong. The anger and the pain kept me in the fight as we rolled and struggled along the river bank.

God: You are the worst pantywaist I've ever seen! You are a daisy!

Jacob: In the middle of a fight, have you ever had someone say something that was so outrageous that it struck you funny? A daisy! That was so silly I broke out in uncontrollable laughter, so uncontrollable that I couldn't fight. The stranger also got to laughing so hard he stopped fighting, too.

It took a long time, but finally we began to get our breath back. We just lay exhausted on the ground, watching as the eastern sky began to glow with the coming morning.

God: Time to go.

Jacob: Hey, wait a minute. What was all that insulting and the put-downs all about?

God: I figured if I put you down far enough, you'd realize you weren't as bad as all that.

Jacob: Yah, but the fight!

God: You had a lot of anger to get worked out of your system.

Jacob: I'm pretty strong and you got me so angry with that rock on my hip and all your insults, I might have torn you apart.

God: I don't do this with everyone who is as low as you were.

Jacob: Who are you?

God: Who are you?

Jacob: Jacob.

God: That's worth something. Isaac and Rebekah were your parents. Isaac, the loyal one, the blind one. Rebekah, the quick-witted one, the unscrupulous one. And Abraham and Sarah were your grandparents, Abraham the faithful, fearful one. And Sarah, the hospitable and jealous one.

Jacob: So I come from a mixed bag.

God: But you can choose from the mix that you are. Take the blessings and practice them. You don't have to be blind, unscrupulous, fearful, and jealous. As the old-timers say, "Trust God to do what he can with a man who limps."

Jacob: Suddenly he was gone. I unloaded the rocks and limped across the ford. Rachel and Joseph were waiting just past the top of the bank on the other side.

Rachel: When you didn't come, we came back to find you. Jacob, your robe is all torn and dirty and wet. Are you all right?

Jacob: Except for a very sore hip, I'm okay. God came and gave me a very unusual blessing last night. Let me tell you about it.

The lameness stayed with me the rest of my life and reminded me of the night-wrestler. I would never walk in lofty arrogance again. I beheld myself as others saw me that night. They say the soul must contend with the one to whom it is accountable. There finally is no greater blessing that we can receive, even if we come out limping.

Comment: I have no better excuse for including this story sermon than that I like it. It uses a third person, by means of his journal, to tell the story of Joseph meeting his brothers in Egypt years after they had sold him into slavery. Since the narrative has similarities to the previous story of Jacob, a creative pastor might want to use the radio drama format.

Churches with closed circuit television might want to experiment with further dramatization, costumes, and sets. One of the great qualities of storytelling is that it opens up vistas of opportunity to engage others, church members and non-church members alike, in the creative process of preaching.

By the way, the "fight" scene described in the story actually occurred. A young church member successfully defended himself in the Rock County (Wisconsin) jail back in 1970.

Joseph's Pit
Genesis 37:2-8

Slaves aren't suppose to be able to write. Hebrews aren't supposed to know about anything but sheep, according to the nations of the world. So my ability, as a Hebrew, to write was so unlikely that no one noticed my practice of keeping a diary here in Egypt. Except Joseph. He doesn't miss much. When Pharoah made him Prime Minister at the age of thirty, he needed someone who could write and keep accurate records. That is how I got on his staff.

How did he know? When we first met twenty years ago, we were both being taken to Egypt by some Ishmaelite traders to be sold as slaves. Being the same age, we stuck together as long as we could. The second morning after he joined the caravan, he whispered to me he knew I could write.

"How do you know?" I asked. I was so startled I almost choked. You see, I hadn't done any writing since I entered the caravan the week before. Writing frightens most strangers and I wasn't about to get anyone down on me.

"It was easy to tell," Joseph said quietly. "When people sleep, their eyes and mouths move. In your case, I also noticed that your fingers moved."

I don't know which was the greater surprise, his knowing I could write or his not being bitter about becoming a slave. Let me say a word about how he came to be in our caravan.

He told me how he grew up in a large, wealthy family. He has ten older brothers, but his father favored him.

"I guess I was spoiled," he told me. "My older brothers resented me as long as I can remember. I don't know whether my parents favored me from the beginning or whether they felt they had to make up for my brothers' envy. But I got whatever I wanted. I thought that was great! Except it was lonely. If it had not been for my younger brother, Benjamin, my loneliness would have been terrible. We both were born of Rachel. The others were born of our other three mothers."

Joseph told me of some of the things that aggravated the older brothers, especially the dreams where they would some day bow down to him like they would to a king. Even his father was upset with that!

As I started to say, Joseph was taken by his brothers and sold into slavery. He spent the better part of a day in a dry well, a dark pit, knowing his brothers hated him.

I'd have gone crazy down there, but he apparently didn't. I know how bitter I was when I was sold by my uncle. But Joseph showed no bitterness. He said God was helping him get away from his hateful brothers. I wouldn't have believed him, but he was cheerful and alert from the moment I met him. The slave master put him with me because I had been so angry. He thought Joseph would cheer me up, and he did. I believe in God, too. But I never have quite gotten over my anger toward my uncle. It was a real surprise to see how Joseph was taking his involuntary servitude.

I lost track of Joseph after the slave sales at Alexandria. Joseph went early in the trading, being so cheerful and full of life. I thought I was better-looking and smarter, but he could smile easier. Smiles always make homely people like him look good. And I still wasn't smiling.

The last I knew, Joseph was sold to Potiphar, who was responsible for Pharaoh's secret service. I guess I lucked out, surly as I was at the time. The Pharaoh's baker bought me and I went to work in his kitchen.

I was there for eleven years and bored silly for every single day. Joseph says God was with me too or I'd have gone over the wall and been hunted down as a runaway. What saved my sanity was calculating the amounts of yeast it took to leaven which kinds of breads, how long, and under what conditions. That worked for the first few years, but even that got boring. Perhaps the routine finally held me in place. I guess the friendship with the other guys at work, their joking around, their being bored, too, made things bearable.

I take too long to get to my story. Just a quick word about how I rejoined Joseph. When my boss was executed by the Pharoah, our kitchen group was all very anxious. There was a series of people who tried to be head baker. After two years of that, one baker decided to get rid of us before we drove him crazy. Within the hour, all eighteen of us were in the slave market again. Just before the trading was to start, I saw a man about my age talking with each of the slaves. When he got to me, this very official-looking person turned out to be Joseph. This former slave bought me on the spot, even before trading opened.

It was two days before I saw him again. At first, he didn't recognize that I was the one in the caravan with him.

"Jabez, I should have realized!" he said when I was brought in.

"Here I thought you were redeeming an old friend," I said with a trace of bitterness. He came over to me and embraced me.

"If I had known, you would have been by my side from the moment I got you. I didn't recognize you in that baker's uniform," he replied.

"Why then did you take me?" I asked.

"There is a small callous on your second finger. You still write, I see. And I need scribes desperately."

Over the next nine years, I have worked my way up to chief steward with Joseph. We have the responsibility of keeping accounts on and distribution of the grain we have stored during seven very good years. The drought of the last two years has brought people from all parts of the world here to get food. I understand it was Joseph who saw this coming and Pharoah put him in charge. Despite the pressure and the logistical difficulties we've faced these last nine years, Joseph has been his cheerful, enthusiastic self. He really had control of the situation — until several months ago.

That's when a small group of Hebrews came down looking to buy food. Joseph really stiffened up. I've never seen him so edgy. I thought at first it was exhaustion catching up with him. In fact, he did retire early that night and was much more himself the next day. But he still acted strangely. He had me hide the men's payment in the grain sacks we sold them. Then he was overheard by my assistant as accusing them of being spies and taking one of them as a hostage. He then released the others, ordering that additional food be sent home with them so they wouldn't need to open the grain sacks. Strange man!

I asked him about it that night. Even though I was technically a slave, Joseph treated us all as co-workers, and spoke to us as peers, even as friends. "Jabez, I don't know what is happening. I thought I was over all the anger and bitterness, but I haven't been too clear on what I was doing these last three days."

"Are you bitter about your prison experience?" I asked. Joseph, you see, had spent several years in prison. His first master's wife had accused him of attacking her and he was jailed on account of it. I thought he had run into some pretty bad experiences and was just now reacting to all of that.

"No, that's not it. Oh, it was bad, all right. Don't get me wrong. I remember one night before lockup, an indurate malefactor — he was the hardest of the criminals there. Some words, huh? — came into my cell. I was as tall and almost as heavy as he was, but I was quiet and didn't cause any trouble, stayed pretty much to myself at the time. Anyway, this troublemaker came in and started to make obscene advances. Usually, I can talk my way out of trouble, but I couldn't say anything, I was so scared.

" 'Oh God,' I thought, 'what do I do now?'

"The man laughed at me.

" 'Prayin' to your God?' he sneered and laughed again.

"I caught him in the chest just above his belly. Hit him just right. He fell backwards through the door into the cell across the way. It was over that quick. He just sat there looking at me.

" 'Good night,' I said to him, and I smiled. I went over to my bed and nearly fainted. I wasn't hurt. He wasn't hurt. But no one took a chance with me after that," Joseph ended his story.

"But you surely must have been affected by that time in jail. You were there unfairly, I understand," I went on.

"No, interestingly, as bad as that place was, I got along with everyone. I was in prison, but I was still free inside myself. I could have let the terror and loneliness of the place shape me, but I decided a long time ago to look for the vitality, the good things that that place offered me. Once in a while it got me down, but I found out most of the prisoners were interesting. I learned a lot about human nature, what goes on in politics, how to do a lot of different things. Want to know how to make cheese or break into a house? I learned it all."

"Well," I asked, "what did you experience that made you act so strange with those men from Canaan?"

"They're my brothers," he said. "As I sat down with them, I found myself so glad to see them I could hardly stand it and at the same time, I was in that dry well, that dark, frightening hole they threw me in. I thought I was going crazy."

"What are your plans now?" I asked.

"I don't know. It would be good to just forget everything and stay away from them. I don't like that awful anger and fear that hit me when I was with them."

"But you can't ignore them. You still have Simeon as a hostage."

"I know," he said. And he stopped talking. He sat there a long time. And then he said, "Good night." He wasn't smiling. So I left.

I asked him about it several times since, but he avoided the subject. Once, he said God would be with us in whatever happened. But that was it. Although I knew it worried him, I was glad to see him enter his work with the old gusto. He asked me to see to Simeon's well-being, but he stayed away and warned me not to say anything.

Two days ago, the brothers came back. Again they didn't recognize Joseph. It had been so long since they had seen him, and, besides, we wear a lot of make-up. They also didn't know that Joseph and I knew Hebrew. We used interpreters with all foreigners. But I recognized them. And I realized they had brought Benjamin along. From the way they talked, they were afraid something would happen to him. They even worked out a way to stand and to walk around Benjamin so that no one would spear him or shoot an arrow at him without first hitting one of them.

When Joseph saw his brothers he nearly fell apart. The make-up covered up his feelings, but I could tell. He asked me to take them to his house for dinner and he left the room hurriedly.

At dinner, he sat at his table and left the brothers to a table of their own. He saw to it that Benjamin got all the best of it, but everyone had plenty. Then he called me over and gave me orders to pack their grain plus a little extra, a silver cup to go into Benjamin's bag.

"Why?" I asked.

"Maybe they need to learn a little lesson or two," he said. When he had that look and that tone of voice, I didn't like him very well.

Today, when everyone was packed, including Simeon, we sent them on their way. They had wondered why they found their money the first time. I told them that God must have put it here, because I had recorded their payment.

Just after they left, Joseph sent guards out after them to search for the silver cup. They came back and Joseph met them. He was like a bear. It turned my stomach.

"How could you be so ungrateful," he cried. "I'll take the guilty one and make him my slave!"

The brothers dissolved in frustration and anger. Their youngest brother, Ben, hadn't been released by Jacob, their father, except for dire concern: hunger.

Judah, speaking for the brothers, offered himself in place of Benjamin. He told of how the death of another brother, Joseph, long ago had nearly killed their father. This would surely do it, if Benjamin were imprisoned in Egypt.

As Judah spoke, Joseph began to change. He grabbed a towel, took off his hat, wiped the make-up off his face, and said, tears streaming from his eyes, "Judah, Simeon, Benjamin, Reuben, I am your brother Joseph."

There was a moment of shock; then the unbelievable relief that went through the room nearly shook it apart. They were all crying and hugging and pounding each other on the back.

That night, after everyone was asleep, with the peace that passes understanding holding them cradled for the first time in years, Joseph sat up awake and, surprisingly, unsure of himself.

"I couldn't string it out. I wanted them to feel guilty. I wanted them to hate themselves for hurting me. I wanted them to know the fear of that pit that they left me in. But I couldn't do it. I couldn't take the hurt I saw when all I was asking was to have my own brother stay. Revenge is not sweet. It's as bitter as any anger I ever felt. But did I do right?" Joseph asked me.

"Our God is the only one who is allowed to take revenge, not us," were the words that came out. "Love is sweet, not vengeance."

He looked at me, and said, "It was terrible in that pit. I don't know why I thought it was worth making anyone else go through it."

Comment: It was Labor Day weekend and it was also a time when I found myself involved in a bit of a confrontation with some leaders in my Annual Conference. That led to a strange combination. But knowing the story of Moses and realizing that he undertook the mission to free his people, I found myself putting together the few bits of data about Moses' wife in all that and came up with a fictitious correspondence.

It was easy to find a reader for the Zipporah part because the church had a number of women who would read it well. The first time I tried it, the reader got it at the beginning of the service. I did it three years later and the reader had several days to look at it. In neither case did we practice together. But the reader's sense of timing was just fine. In both cases, the reader read from the back of the nave.

Moses' New Job
Exodus 4:24-26, 18:2-9

My dearest Zipporah,

He came. Just as God promised, Aaron came. It is all falling into place. God is with me in this new venture. Aaron came yesterday and told me how God had come to him in a dream and that he, Aaron, should come to meet me. No one knew I was heading for Egypt except you and your father. So I don't know how else Aaron would know to come than by the grace of God.

As excited as I am now about our mission, I must tell you how lonely it is since you returned to your father's house. Those first few weeks after you left, I thought I would go crazy. At night, my body ached for you. During the day, I felt like I was going in circles around the hole that was left in my life by your leaving. So many times I thought I heard Gershom call to me, and I'd look and look … And then I'd be crushed not to see him … or you.

I've been beside myself worrying about how the birthing has gone. Your being great with child was one of the reasons I felt you were right in going back with your father's messenger. My mission is not what is helpful to a birthing mother. Oh, may our God watch over you and protect you and the new baby boy.

Aaron is here and we will be in Goshen by the end of the month.

Your loving husband,
Moses

To Moses, the messenger of God,

My beloved, why didn't you write sooner? I've been frantic about you and your newest crusade. Why don't you just come back and not try to be the great hero? There's plenty to do here. Dad's sheep need care. The other sons-in-law are not that much help. If you want to do something important, you can run for tribal council or handle petitions against modern deadly weapons. Why do you have to take on Capitol Hill?

Your worried wife,
Zipporah

Sent by my father's messenger

Dear Zipporah,

I thought you knew. I thought I went over everything before we started out together. Let me tell you again.

You know I'm Hebrew. You know the story about how my mother saved my life in a time when the Pharoah wanted all male Hebrew babies killed, how she put me in a reed basket and floated me down the river to where the Pharaoh's daughter was swimming, and how she had my sister offer my mother's services as wetnurse and maid for me when Pharaoh's daughter decided to keep me.

You know how I grew up, trained in our religion, language, and culture by my mother and trained also in Egyptian life and ways by the princess. I was very fond of her and she was nice to me, but we never were close. You know how her death at the hands of the new Pharoah caught us all by surprise. Why he didn't come after me at the same time I'll never know. But such injustice burned me very deeply.

I saw that injustice again when the foreman overseeing a group of my Hebrew relatives struck down one of them for no reason. The others ran, but I tackled the foreman. Maybe I was angry about Pharaoh's injustice, too. All I know is, I got up after fighting and the foreman didn't. He was dead. I buried him in the sand and carried the injured relative who was still unconscious back to the camp. I was still upset over the foreman's cruelty and over what I saw in the camp, the bitterness, the despair, the slum conditions of the families. It was bad. I knew I had to do something. Now is my chance. And, God is with me!

Your husband,
Moses

Dear Moses, Prophet of the Lord,

Your God! Your obsession. You were so caught up in your crusade that you dreamt one night your God was attacking you. Remember that? It was so real to you that you screamed out to me to circumcise Gershom. You weren't able to settle down until I finally did it. That was such a bad night! I'll never forget it.

What kind of religion is it that so distorts a man's emotions that even his dreams become so awful? How can you be confident you are doing right in trying to be the savior of your people? You're part of us now and you have had nothing to do with the Hebrews for years. Please do not go any further. We need you here.

Sincerely,
Zipporah

Sent by my father's messenger

Dearest Zipporah,

I don't want to be here. I'm no savior. I'm no hero. God surely knows. After I killed that foreman, I ended up running away and hiding. That's when I came to the well where I met you and your sisters.

You remember how when I first started out as a shepherd for your father, I used to have hallucinations. You and your sisters had to come and find me several times because I had forgotten to drink water and would eventually wander in circles, babbling out of my mind. It would only take a day or so in the heat of the Midian desert pastures. I wasn't used to the climate.

Well, three months ago, when I was with the sheep, I began to feel like the hallucinations were starting again. But I had been very careful about the water. Yet, I saw the burning bush.

I told you about that at the time. I couldn't believe my eyes.

But then, my ears began, too. I heard a voice call to me from that odd bush. When I went closer, I found myself talking to God. It wasn't the same as at prayer time. It was so real! I covered my face and head with my robe, I was so frightened.

But the voice persisted, loud and clear, even though with my head and ears covered I could not see or hear anything else.

The voice told of the affliction of my people in Egypt. The voice proclaimed to be the God of Abraham, Isaac, and Jacob, and that the promise still held that we would go back to the land of Israel. And then the voice said, "You will bring them out."

"Do you know who you are asking?" I said as I unwrapped the cloak. I looked around but could only see the strange bush. The voice came from it again.

"You and I make a majority. I'm not talking to someone else. If I wanted someone else, do you think I'd be wasting my time here? You are the one. I WILL BE WITH YOU," the voice said.

"Where were you when I killed the Egyptian foreman?" I asked.

The voice responded, "I did what I had to do. You remember that Pharoah failed to come after you after the princess was killed. And you now have had experience in this desert area. You'll bring them out through these places and Pharaoh's armies will not follow you here."

"If you can do all that, why don't YOU bring them out?" I asked.

"This is too big a project. I've been having to take it a little at a time. And you're one of the pieces in this puzzle," the voice came back.

"Even if I try it, no one's going to believe me. They'll think I'm desert crazy. For instance, who will I say is the God involved?"

"I AM WHO I AM!" the voice said.

"So I am who I am," I answered. "I can't do this savior stuff. You saw me run," I told this God.

"Listen, there are no other Gods more important. I am the one who put this world together and I'm tired of all this chicken stuff from you. Now you are going to do it, and when they ask you who is behind you, tell them it is the one in all the universe that knows what is what and who is who. I set it up so you and everybody else can either dig in on history or cop out and let the world fall apart because you are too busy or too chicken. I had to go after Abraham, Isaac, and Jacob to move things along. And I did. Now it's your turn."

"Can you give me some kind of miracle to use to show that You have some power in this situation?" I asked.

85

"I'll give you two tricks. They may impress people. Maybe they won't. But don't count on them. People will figure it's magic."

To make a long story short, He took none of my excuses. God promised to send Aaron, my older brother, to work with me. And Aaron's here with me. And we are going on.

I miss you very much. I'm still very afraid.

Love,
Moses

To Moses, the Crusader for the great I AM,

Your long letter still leaves me very uneasy. It could just be a coincidence that Aaron came out to meet you. You're right. Your conversation with God sounds like desert-crazy talk. Please come back before it is too late. We still need you.

Your wife,
Zipporah

Sent by my father's messenger

Dear Zipporah,

Aaron and I met with the Hebrew leaders today. They took my word for it that God will help them escape their slavery.

It is terrible here. There are mostly men older than me. The boy-child killing backfired on Pharoah. So he quit after twenty years, realizing he was depleting his labor force. He has put women to work. He has cut water and food rations. He's become paranoid about the Hebrews. If he keeps up the harassing and the assassinations, there won't be a nation for God to give as a blessing to the world. We plan no military attacks. We plan no retaliation. We plan to exit this place as gracefully and low-key as possible. Pharoah may not cooperate. But we have made up our minds. Everyone is gathering up jewelry, food, clothing, anything we can use to make the trip across the desert to where we can settle down away from slavery, away from this tyranny.

When I saw all the hardship and got the immediate support of the Hebrew leaders, I really felt that desert talk with God was true. Even if it was a crazy dream, it got me out of my mid-life lethargy and has given me something I can give my life for. I'm glad you are safe. Oh, my, the baby! Was it born all right? Are you all right? I almost forgot! Answer quickly.

All my love,
Moses

Dearest Moses,

Father finally let me send a letter by my messenger instead of by his. Now I can tell you that he made me leave you. I would be there by your side, except he watches me constantly. I know he is worried about me and the birthing, and I know he is fully aware of the danger you are in. But he underestimates my courage and my strength. He, like most men, doesn't realize what it takes to have a baby. Talk about labor! I'm sorry. I want to be with you. We will join you as soon as I can persuade my father.

The birthing went fine. You wanted a boy and you have a boy. He is doing very well. Gershom is a lot of help. We would have done well WITH you, too. But we weren't given that chance.

Forgive the tone of my questions in these past letters. I know your longing for using all your skills. I know your energy and what it can bring about. But I had to slow you down so that you could be sure. I knew from the start, but I also knew your doubts about yourself. Besides, if I had encouraged you too much, my father would have cut off the correspondence.

Please know you go with my blessing. May God go before you by day and be with you by night. May Pharoah not hold you back. May you have courage, the staying power, to be God's person, no matter what happens.

All my love and respect,
Your Zipporah

Comment: Having focused on doing story sermons during one summer, all fall I missed the creativity I had felt. When Christmastime came around, the urge hit me again. Some years earlier, I had done a Christmas story (see the next story sermon) and so I decided to try it again.

What really happened Christmas Day? Who took care of the sheep while the shepherds went to town? What happened to Joseph and Mary and the baby? How did they get into a house where the Wisemen were to find them several days later?

Our congregation was becoming accustomed to my practice of having a hymn sing every few months during the regular worship service. At Christmastime, there is rarely enough time to sing all of the carols the congregation wants to sing, so I scheduled a carol sing for the Sunday after Christmas. One of the pillars of the church said she enjoyed the singing, but always felt a little empty if there wasn't a story or something, so the following was my offering that Sunday.

WHAT REAlly HAppENEd CHRiStMAS DAy
LukE 2:8-20

"It's almost dawn and they still aren't back," Matthal mumbled to himself. The sheep were beginning to stir and he'd have his hands full trying to keep them together if the shepherds didn't get back pretty soon.

A lamb bleated on the far side of the flock. Matthal strained to see what had startled it. "The wolves are usually bedded down by now," he thought to himself. Then he realized that the road to Bethlehem lay just beyond where the sound came from.

"Just in time! They're back," he said out loud.

Then he heard them singing a psalm as they walked along. He hadn't heard them sound so religious since Passover. He wasn't so sure their singing was a good sign. At the holiday, they had a little too much to drink, tried to get everyone at the inn to sing a psalm, got to feeling they could clear out the whole Roman army, and started after a couple soldiers who were off duty. Fortunately, the soldiers kept their cool and talked the shepherds down out of their drunken enthusiasm. No, the singing was definitely not a good sign to Matthal.

When the shepherds saw the flock, they split up to take their normal stations for the morning chores. Jerod came over to Matthal.

"Thank you for watching the flock for us. We'll never forget what happened to us tonight, never!" Jerod gushed.

"Glad to help," Matthal replied. "You took off in such a hurry after getting me out here that you didn't even say what this was all about."

"We didn't think you'd believe us and we weren't sure whether we believed it ourselves; but we found the baby just like the angels told us, and, by God, we think he's the Messiah!" Jerod overflowed.

"Wait a minute," Matthal said, trying to build up the dike so he wouldn't be washed away. "Try that on me again."

"Just as the sheep were finally settled down for the night, we heard this fantastic-looking ... angel. I never saw one before, but there it was ... And the place began to glow. Fortunately, the ... angel ... didn't stir up the sheep. But he ... she ... it stirred us up, scared us half to death! Then he told us not to be scared but to listen. He told us a baby had been born in Bethlehem that would be the Messiah. And there was this choir of angels ..." Jerod flowed on.

"Jerod," Matthal interrupted, "if I had known you were getting me out of bed so that you could go out on a toot, I would have..."

"No, nothing like that! Well, maybe we had an extra taste of wine after supper ... but even if we were drunk, and the angels weren't real ... I think they were ... we were so shaken by their coming ... to us! Who are we? Nobodies! But they came and they said to go ... so we went. And we found the baby boy, just like they said. That baby was real and so was the stable we were told to head for. What a thrill! I still can't get over it! The Messiah is finally here!"

"A baby," Matthal muttered. No, the Messiah would come on a donkey, would ride it into Jerusalem, would lead a mighty army against Rome. No, no baby. That would be so useless.

As Matthal thought, Jerod babbled on about the young mother and father, how they were strangers, how they came for the census, about their dreams of angels talking to them about the baby. Matthal suddenly became aware of Jerod's cascading and interrupted him.

"Are they still there?" he asked.

"Who, the angels?" Jerod replied.

"No, the young couple."

"I guess so. We were so excited, we had to tell everybody. So we left, but so far, you are the only one we've found awake. Wait till we get these sheep back to the fold. Maybe now someone will pay attention to us. The Messiah is born! WOW!"

"Jerod," Matthal brought his friend back down to earth. "It's late and I've been up most of the night so ..."

"Oh, here let me pay you for watching the sheep." Jerod pulled out a little coin and handed it to Matthal so that he could go home and get some rest.

Matthal took the denarius and headed for town. Even though the thought of his bed pulled him toward his home, he headed toward the inn. When he got to the stable next to the inn, he found everyone was asleep. Rather than wake them, he found a spot in the hay and rested there.

"Mary, look what we have here. It appears to be another of those shepherds."

The voice of the young man woke Matthal. The sun was up and his stomach was feeling very empty. It took him a moment to realize where he was.

"Oh, I'm sorry," he said to the young man. "I don't mean to impose. My friends told me this incredible story last night. They were so caught up in it that they forgot their manners. Welcome to Bethlehem. Where are you from? How are the mother and the baby? How come you are in the stable?" He began to feel like his friend Jerod the way the words came tumbling out. He blushed with his feeling so foolish.

The young man waited him out just as though it was the most natural thing in the world. He reached down, pulled Matthal up onto his feet.

"My name is Joseph. Because of the census, we had to come back here to my ancestral village. We got in late, the inn was full, but the stable was available. We have had worse places to stay on our way down here, so we accepted. Then the baby came."

As he spoke, Matthal marveled at his calm. He was also glad not to hear all that religious stuff.

Matthal did not think of himself as religious. He never went to Minyan. Even when the men needed him to make up the ten required by law for the worship service, Matthal felt it was hypocritical to sit in on the prayers and the Messiah talk that always followed. He had not learned that much at synagogue. He seldom got there after bar mitzvah. His dad and the rabbi had disagreed about something, so his dad always had found some important chore for Matthal to do whenever it was time to go to synagogue. He'd sneak off and meet his buddies there anyway in order to hear the scroll read and to get the free lunch afterward, but he got home in a hurry to finish the chore before his dad realized he was gone. So much for his religion.

"Joseph, again I apologize. I came so I could help you find someplace else to stay besides here in a stable. I couldn't believe Jerod didn't think of it. Do you have anyplace else here?"

"No, we're from Nazareth and we haven't been here before."

"Do you know of any relatives?"

"I'm sure there's somebody, but I haven't any idea who that might be. We don't know of anyone in our parents' families who actually lives here."

Matthal, feeling frustrated, tried to think of some way to get a clue that could help him.

"Joseph, how far back can you go with your family tree?" He felt he had something.

"Let's see, my father was Heli. My grandfather's name was Matthal. He was descended from Levi who was the son of ... of what's his name ...?"

"Could it have been Melchi?"

"Yes, how did you know?"

"A lot of the folks here are related one way or another. My great-grandfather was Levi and my great-great-grandfather was Melchi. I remember my father saying he had an uncle who moved up north. I was named after him. My name is Matthal too."

"That makes you second cousins." The voice was that of the young mother, Mary. She had just changed the cloth on the baby and was bringing him over to show him to Matthal.

He actually found himself looking for a halo or something around the baby's head. The way Jerod had talked, he was sure there was something unusual. But there wasn't, only the normal, red, wrinkled face of a newborn. His eyes didn't focus. Nothing, just a baby.

"Matthal?"

Joseph was trying to get his attention.

"Yes," he replied immediately, embarrassed at his thoughts.

"He's only a baby and we know that. Your shepherd friends really made a big fuss. It was hard to keep them from being so excited."

"Did you smell the wine?"

Matthal couldn't believe he had said that.

93

"Yes," said Joseph, "but they were okay. They didn't really bother us. It had been pretty lonely 'til they came. Only one maid from the inn came to help as midwife and she had to go back in to take care of the other guests once the baby was born."

"Hey, I came to help you find a place to stay. Now that we know we are related, I think I can do something about it. First, though, you must come and have a meal with me. I live alone and have only a small room, but we can eat outside in the shade. How's your water holding up? Can I get some for you? I'm sorry. There I go again."

"That's okay. We need the water. The innkeeper is rationing his water because of the overcrowding."

"I'll be back in a few minutes. You get your things together. But first the water. Then the meal. Then I'll get you a decent place."

"You're not very religious, are you?" Joseph observed.

"You need that water. We can talk over lunch," Matthal said as he started for the door.

"Matthal, don't worry about it ... the observation I made. Not everyone has visions and says prayers and does all the religious things. I really think that the ones who welcome the stranger, who feed the hungry, who give water to the thirsty, I think God wants that from us more than anything else," Joseph said.

"Aw, teach it to your boy," Matthal said flippantly as he turned to go. As he went out the door, he hoped Joseph would.

Comment: This was the first story sermon for adults that I wrote and dramatized during worship. I had written a number of story sermons for children, but the breakthough came because an old sermon I had been revising every half-dozen years was not taking shape. I started to write. Usually, I have just outlined sermons and "talked" them to the congregation. When I got started on this one, I found a text forming with which I decided to stay.

There were two major problems that I had with this one. The most important was the fact that I was bound to the text and read it. The people were unaccustomed to that and did not really like it. So, I opened with an introduction in my normal style to establish why I was reading the story! Second, to try to minimize the "reading" feel of the story, I worked on differing voices for the various characters. And I had quite a few! I discovered I was not as talented at that as the readers on the state radio network's "Chapter a Day" program.

Here is a good example of why a story sermon from someone else's hand will never be as good as your own in your own church!

The Wisemen
Matthew 2:1-12

I hate it when Christmas is over. There's so much good music, such tasty foods, so much color and warmth. And presents! I love presents! I wish we celebrated all twelve days of Christmas.

I could be dissuaded from that last enthusiasm if it meant that I would be given all the presents from that funny Christmas carol:

22 turtle doves
30 French hens
36 calling birds
40 gold rings
42 geese a'laying
42 swans a'swimming
40 maids a'milking
36 ladies dancing
30 lords a'leaping
22 pipers piping
12 drummers drumming
and 12 partridges in a pear tree

Giving of presents and the twelve days of Christmas are traditionally tied to the coming of the three wisemen.

There are a lot of stories written about them. I've tried my hand at it.

Picture, if you will, three learned men, professors, scholars. Don't forget, while most of our European ancestors were still scratching out a living farming or fishing, the Middle East had extensive art, literature, and culture. There were many great universities and libraries.

In my story, Caspar is the eldest, a professor of philosophy from India. Melchior, the youngest, is an astronomer from Arabia. Balthazar is a mathematics teacher from Ethiopia.

Tradition has it that these three met at the city of Petra, one hundred miles south of Jerusalem, to share a journey in search of a new Jewish king. The main clue that they had to his existence was an unusual star. Such a search against great odds, reported in only one place (the star), does not exactly excite the intellectual community. In fact, most of us, given a newspaper account rather than a Bible telling, would probably have laughed at them, if we had noticed the article in the first place. But since the story is told in the Bible, we read it and find little reason to doubt it. And so the three Wisemen of the east, immortalized in carol and Christmas pageant, wend their way through our imaginations to the stable the night of the Christ child's birth, or as other traditions say, some twelve days later to the house in Bethlehem where the young family went before their sudden departure for Egypt. The presents brought by these teachers turn out to be necessary for the survival of the family.

There are many ideas and values that we can find in this ancient story, but let me, in my telling, try to discover the nature of their wisdom so that we might become more wise ourselves.

The three men were resting that first night after they started their journey.

"Did your colleagues give you a bad time?" Caspar asked.

"I expected a lot more difficulty than they actually gave me. The worst I got," Balthazar responded, "was that I was going out of my field. My political science colleagues at the university thought it was foolish for a mathematician to embark on a visit with a king."

Melchior looked pained. The other two waited for him to speak. "The faculty at my school have barred me from further teaching there. With my life's savings tied up in this trip, I have nothing to which to go back. They couldn't believe I had no interest in measuring movements of the strange star and recording the data in a professional journal. Publish, publish, publish! That's all they think of! Don't take a chance, don't risk anything, don't give up your seniority or security unless you can get ahead. It is frightening to me how they see the intellectual task. No wonder our schools turn out so many students with dead curiosity, with little creativity, with no sense of the wonder and mystery in the world around them."

"You sound almost relieved, my brother," Caspar observed.

"Frightened, Caspar," he responded, "frightened. It has been my only position for ten years. Right now I don't feel very wise at all."

"My co-workers were neither unconcerned nor antagonistic. One friend said he would have sent a graduate student to do the research! Another would have taken expensive equipment to study the meteorology. Yet another would have had a dozen team members from different disciplines, like a medical person, a sociologist, even a physical therapist to rub his sore muscles! But none even considered coming. They couldn't imagine anything significant in the very small event of a birth of a king of a nondescript tribe." Thus Caspar described his experience.

"Do you still see any significance, now that you have put your money out for this search and left the comfort of your warm office at the university?" Melchior asked.

"Yes, I still do," Caspar replied.

"After a couple more days on these camels you may not," Balthazar joked.

The men turned to checking their star charts and maps to be sure that the track they had projected would get them past the dry, waterless terrain ahead before their supplies ran out for that section of their journey. Then they rested.

Several days later they were about six miles south of Jerusalem.

"Brothers, according to my calculations, the new king will be found just a little west of here," Balthazar asserted.

"But Jerusalem is the capital city. What king would be born away from there? It has the families bearing the royal blood. It has all the comforts that kings do not seem to be able to do without. In fact, I'd like some of them myself right now," Caspar teased. "Seriously," he went on, "it seems more plausible to go to Jerusalem. Not having your mathematical skills, I cannot check your figures, but all the other signs of the presence of the new king seem to point to the city," he concluded.

Melchior joined in. "I trust your calculations, my friend, but I, too, am confused by their proximity to the city, which would seem a more appropriate site. Since we are so close to the city anyway,

Balthazar, perhaps we can learn something to either refine your figures or clear up our objections."

And so the three scholars, experts in the properties of nature, and yet struggling as you or I over the handling of disagreements, headed for Jerusalem.

On the road, a small contingent of soldiers came in their direction from the city. Upon inquiry, the Wisemen not only got directions on how to get to a suitable hospice for the night, they also got a military escort. The young lieutenant explained that there were robbers who mugged anyone who came along those roads, and so the king himself had requested the guard for their protection.

The men felt honored indeed. And they were even more impressed when the soldiers took them directly to the capitol building. After they were given opportunity to clean up and eat, they were invited to talk with the king himself, again quite an honor.

"Politicians don't always care to hear from university professors," observed Balthazar.

"Neither do other university professors," quipped Caspar.

"Does anyone?" wondered Melchior.

"Our mystics tell us that you are on a significant research project," the King opened.

"We think so," replied Caspar.

"They sense that it has something to do with a king," their host went on. "Is it perhaps ourselves?"

"Sir, according to our best calculations, we will not be in the presence of the king we seek until we get a little beyond the southern suburbs of Jerusalem," Balthazar reported. "Say, how did your mystics know . . ." he began.

The king interrupted.

"Well, if there is another king, we are most anxious to join you in your quest and to meet him. But if you are correct in your analysis of the figures and he is not here, perhaps our scholars can come up with something. Let us continue our conversations in the morning." With that, the King smiled, and left the room. The three men silently watched him go.

"That was good of him," Balthazar said to the others.

"I'm glad to get the help, too," Caspar said. "But there are some things that don't fit. He was so swift in cutting you off when you wanted to ask him how his mystics function."

"Yes, and did you feel he was sincere about wanting to go? I thought I was scared before about this trip, but I feel some new fear and I don't know for sure why," added Melchior.

His colleagues did not let themselves be bothered by his feelings. While they mostly relaxed, they respected their partner's different reaction to the situation.

The next morning, the king called the three scholars before him and shared some good news. "Your mathematician friend has properly calculated. Our historians have researched the holy writings and similarly contend that the village of Bethlehem, just a few miles southwest of here, is the proper place for a new king to be found. King David, our ancestral predecessor, came from there and the mystics of old say another will come from there one day."

"How do you mathematicians do it?" Melchior queried. And the three men laughed heartily.

The king did not quite get the drift of their humor and waited until they composed themselves. "Duties of state require that we stay, but please go, find this new king you say is coming, and let us know where he is so we can go and meet him."

The Wisemen gladly withdrew, still feeling a little strange in the presence of a king, and, in Melchior's case, feeling a little frightened. They left immediately and found their way to Bethlehem.

"According to my calculations, the exact spot is near that inn over there," Balthazar told his friends.

It was late afternoon. So the men thought they would try to stay there for the night, especially if they had found the king.

"Sorry, fellas, there ain't no room here. Didn't you hear about the census? Oh, you ain't from here. How could you know? Anyway, you're out of luck. The place is full up," the innkeeper told them.

"How about your stable?" the men asked.

"You're welcome to it. There ain't no other place in town I know of. That's strange. Almost two weeks ago, I sent a couple in there. No one else has even thought to ask for it," he answered.

"This may sound strange, my friend," Caspar asked of the inn-keeper, "but do you know of any king who is staying here at your inn?" They hadn't forgotten their mission at all. But the unlikeliness of there being a king there was so overpowering that the questions seemed almost ridiculous.

"Ridiculous!" the innkeeper said. "You'll find the king in Jerusalem. King Herod. Yeah, you'll find him in Jerusalem, I hope!"

The three men looked at each other and then headed for the stable.

Just then, a soldier stepped out from the lengthening shadows and stopped them. It was the young lieutenant.

"Did you find the king?" he asked nervously.

"Sorry. The innkeeper laughed at us and thought we were pretty stupid not to be in Jerusalem," Caspar replied.

"After all our travel and after all my calculations and all the help of your king ..." Balthazar began.

"My king," the lieutenant groaned. "Yes, my king. I'm relieved you didn't find anyone here. I would have had to report it and the king would have ordered me to kill the baby king. Thank God you university people were on a wild goose chase! I couldn't have looked at myself if I had to do the king's foul play. Well, gentlemen, thank you for your good news. I'm sorry for you that you didn't succeed."

"Young man," Melchior asked, "how did Herod know our purpose? Are his mystics that sensitive?"

"Well, once in a while they are right. But in this case, he had spies in Petra and they followed you all the way to near Jerusalem because they overheard you sought out a newborn king. They knew Herod would be interested. We were sent out to be sure you didn't get away before we had a chance to interrogate you."

"What about muggers?" Melchior asked.

"Oh, that's the excuse the powers-that-be around here always use to justify what they want to do. There are some, don't get me wrong. But the rumor keeps people afraid so that they don't get out to do anything about the other things wrong around here," he replied candidly. "If you gentlemen will excuse me, I'll take my men and we'll be on our way."

The sun was now set and it was nearly dark as the wisemen got their gear into the stable.

"No king! I can't believe it. All the data points to one being here. Why? What did we do wrong? Was it the young lieutenant? Was the innkeeper lying to us? Is the king around here somewhere only we don't know it? Are we overlooking something in our own data that would be a clue now?" Caspar asked the questions all of them were feeling as the fear of failure began to engulf them.

They were wise enough to accept the possibility that they had failed. But they were also wise enough to stick around a little longer to leave no possibility unchecked.

They worked well into the night, going back over their original sources. They looked at their calculations again. This time, Balthazar went over the math carefully so that his partners could understand what he had done and so they could correct him if possible.

They took a breather after several hours of concentration, having found no resolution to their frustrating situation.

Melchior commented as they went out the door for some air, "You know, when Herod told us that the Jewish scriptures reported that Bethlehem was the place, I remembered how the others at our university would have scoffed. 'Religious writings are pipe dreams, not scholars' materials!' they'd say. Yet, there was a sense of truth that I can't quite describe about the scriptures."

Caspar, the teacher of philosophy, picked up on this. "As one who tries to deal with all things in clear, objective ways, I, too, have dismissed holy writings because they were either subjective or were biased to attempt to prove a point without the needed homework done by the writer. But there are passages of which I could not make sense if I left it at that. Now what I have realized is that those writers were describing their experience. Granted they tried to bias their readers, they still have the right to their perception and to their way of sharing that. And when I find that they describe reality in a way similar to my experience, then I listen. My regard for scriptures is as high as it is for any other serious effort to help me understand life and reality."

Balthazar was not so objective. "When they are true, they're true! When they are not, then I set them aside. When they said 'Bethlehem' this morning, that was all right with me!"

"Astronomer friend, how is your astrology?" Caspar asked Melchior.

"I watch the heavens, I don't read them. But I know a thing or two. Why do you ask?"

"Well, I see that star we used in our calculations, and it isn't where I remembered its being. Does that mean anything? It's over that house over there."

"In the wrong place? That's it! No astrology, brother. That's because our calculations are based on the wrong date. I mean, we are here twelve days late. That's why you see the star out of place. Why didn't we think of that before?" Melchior went on to explain how the wrong date would affect their calculations.

Caspar saw the possibility first. "That couple and the stable. I wonder whether there was anything unusual about them."

Even before he had finished his sentence, the three men were rushing to the innkeeper's door.

"What happened to that young couple that was here two weeks back?" they asked of the man.

He wasn't exactly ready for them. He had had a few too many. "Nuthin'," he said. "Nuthin's happened to 'em."

"You mean they are still here in town?"

"Yah. They moved over to that house across the way after their baby was born."

"Baby? Which house is that again?" they asked excitedly.

"That one, under the bright star to the east."

They hurried across the square, stopped, and went back to their gear to get some things out of their packs. Then, composing themselves, they walked over to the house. There was a light visible through the window, so they knocked quietly at the door.

The young man who answered was a little surprised to see anyone at all, but he seemed accustomed to welcoming strangers into his home. His experience here in Bethlehem had renewed his commitment to deal respectfully with strangers. The home he and his family were in now was the kindness of a distant relative who opened up an old homestead for them until after the census was taken.

The young woman came over and also welcomed them. "How is it that you are here?" she asked.

Caspar responded, "We scholars are accustomed to pursuits that bring life to its highest value. Our curiosity and desire for resolution of data before us draws us to search out that which is true and that which helps all others."

Balthazar went on, "Our different fields of study pointed to the grave need for and the unique possibility of a new kind of leader, one who would not need force, fear, or death to stir humankind, one who would bring about a new era of life in which there would be peace, freedom, respect, honor, and all the other great qualities of which humanity is capable."

"My colleagues took my astronomical and cartological data seriously and accepted my invitation to come in honor of the coming new king," Melchior added. "And now we wish to do that honor in a way that is more than mere words."

And the three professors presented valuable gifts — gold, frankincense, and myrrh.

"But why don't you present these to King Herod?" the young man asked.

"Why must gifts be given to those who already have enough?" was Caspar's reply.

Melchior brought up the subject. "Young friends, we have been warned that King Herod is to be feared. He learned of our research and sent soldiers to follow us. We think he will probably send soldiers back here just in case. If we return as he requested of us, we would jeopardize our lives and be forced either into having to lie about you or endanger you. You must leave the country as quickly as you can. We just happen to be headed south and would welcome your coming with us."

"That might be dangerous for them," Caspar interjected. "They recognize us and would be very suspicious, if in chasing us and finding you with us ..."

"We will find our way," the young man said quietly. "Thank you for warning us and for the thoughtful offer. We will be on our way," he said, as he began to gather their belongings.

The young woman looked at the three men. "You are so convinced that our child is a new king. From where does such wisdom come?"

Caspar, wishing to hurry the family to leave, yet paused to give a thoughtful answer.

"Because we all need one like him."

Comment: As I put this little book together, I have maintained a kind of biblical chronological order for the respective stories. You will note shifting around of dates now, more so than earlier. Themes for the holidays, Labor Day in this case, and purposes seen for the sake of the congregation, are not always orderly!

This particular sermon was influenced by a story I vaguely remember from Sunday School told nearly a half century ago. And it has been enriched by the Middle West's foremost preacher, humorist Garrison Keillor. There are few storytellers his equal. There are many pastors who enjoy the Saturday night monologues of Keillor and draw upon them for insightful stories and good humor.

I like situations which cross age lines, so I was glad when I had a chance to tell a story about Jesus as a boy. I did the following as a storyteller, but I think it would lend itself to having a young boy take part. As I write this, I have one bright-eyed, bushy-tailed ten-year-old in mind who would have been this way, a little too smart, and still a very thoughtful young person. In my next church, I would probably revise the text to allow for the kind of youngster available to handle the part, if I felt I could use this story.

In The Carpenter's Workshop
Matthew 18:23-35

Commentator: It has been a hot day, as one might expect this time of year in the Holy Land. Joseph and his son Jesus are back from the gate where they have spent the two hottest hours of the day, talking with the men.

Joseph: Now when you've got that sanded really smooth, I want you to rub it with your hands. Okay?

Jesus: Okay. Dad, those men really got into an argument over wages, didn't they?

Joseph: They certainly did. I noticed you wanted to say something.

Jesus: I did, but grownups don't even notice us kids. I hope I never get that way.

Joseph: What were you trying to say?

Jesus: A fair wage is one that the workers agree upon with their boss. As long as it isn't cheating the workers or gouging the boss, I think workers don't need to complain if the boss decides to pay someone extra.

Joseph: But is it fair if the boss pays someone who hardly works the same as he pays someone who has worked all day long?

Jesus: Isn't that up to the one who is in charge?

Joseph: But is it fair?

Jesus: They agreed on it. I think the ones who worked all day are just being greedy. God doesn't want that. I'm done with the sanding.

Joseph: Check the other side there. Okay. Start rubbing it with your hands. What do you think God wants?

Jesus: God wants people with thankful hearts and God wants a fair wage.

Joseph: How do you know that is what God wants?

Jesus: The rabbi said so.

Joseph: Does that make it true?

Jesus: What do you mean?

Joseph: The rabbi talked about a man being worth his hire. Maybe the man needs to ask for a raise.

Jesus: But, Dad, it's still true that God doesn't want greed and He does want people to be treated fairly. Remember when Aunt Martha asked you to fix her door?

Joseph: Do I? That was a hard situation. She is such a sweet person and I could hardly say no. But she expected me to do it for nothing because she is my aunt.

Jesus: You looked so funny when you went up to her after you had fixed the door and told her it would cost two denarii. "Honey, you should have told me!" she said.

Joseph: That was embarrassing. I should have said something before I started, but then she would have said, "How can you charge your flesh and blood such high prices?"

Commentator: There was a knock at the door.

Joseph: Come in. What can I do for you?

Stranger: Are you a carpenter?

Jesus: No, we are shepherds and all these shavings are wool.

Joseph: Jesus! You do your work. I'll take care of our customer.

Stranger: I'm planning to build a tower in my vineyard and I need to know how much it will cost.

Joseph: How high? How wide? On a hillside? Tell me all you can about it. Then I can let you know a price.

Commentator: Joseph and the customer go over the details as young Jesus continues to rub with his hands the wood he is working on.

Joseph: Thank you. I'll be back in a minute.

Jesus: Did you hear about the tower that collapsed last week? It killed three workers.

Stranger: That was God punishing them.

Jesus: Really?

Stranger: Why else? Only bad people get punished. Those workers must have been bad people.

Jesus I know some bad people that no tower has fallen on.

Stranger: What did you say? I missed that.

Joseph: It will cost about forty shekels.

Stranger: That much? Hmmm.

Joseph: You can try my friend Abner. He does good work. You need to know what you are getting into.

Commentator: The customer leaves. Joseph turns to his son.

Joseph: What was that all about?

Jesus: He said God caused accidents to kill bad workers. God's not like that, is He? I always thought God was forgiving.

Joseph: How do you know that?

Jesus: Remember the farmer you built the grape arbor for last year? And the trouble he had with his foreman? He was forgiving toward his foreman. But the foreman was not forgiving toward one of the other workers. He should have been.

Joseph: I remember, and I agree with you.

Jesus: I think God is like the farmer.

Joseph: Why isn't God like the foreman?

Jesus: Well ... that's hard, Dad.

Joseph: What is the Great Commandment?

Jesus: Love God.

Joseph: And?

Jesus: Love our neighbor.

Joseph: Okay, why is God like the farmer and not like the foreman?

Jesus: If God wants us to love, then God is already loving toward us.

Joseph: And?

Jesus: Therefore He is forgiving, like the farmer.

Joseph: Very good. You're learning.

Jesus: How's this for rubbing?

Joseph: Keep it up. That has to be very, very smooth.

Jesus: How about giving me a riddle?

Joseph: Let's see ... Once there was a farmer who went out scattering seed. The seed that fell on the path was eaten by the birds. Some fell among the rocks and sprouted but withered in the sun. Seeds among the weeds were choked out before they could grow very much. But there was seed that fell in good earth and it grew thirty to a hundred fold.

Jesus: That's easy. The Word of God does not take root in the busy mind, it has a hard time in shallow minds, it can be run out by greed and fear and such in those who are afraid, and it can grow like crazy when it is heard and really understood. I've heard that one before.

Joseph: Very good. Say, you are almost done there, aren't you?

Jesus: Just time for one more riddle, only make it hard this time.

Joseph: Okay. If it takes 55 yards of pink linen to make a robe for a baby elephant and it takes a flea ten minutes to kick a half-inch hole in a pickle, how old am I?

Jesus: 44.

Joseph: How did you come up with that figure?

Jesus: Your younger brother is 22 and he's only half crazy!

Joseph: I think you are going to have to learn a little respect, my son! But that is a good riddle, isn't it! Now let's see how that cross is coming.

Jesus: Why do we have to be so careful to make it as smooth as possible? The Romans use the crosses to execute criminals.

Joseph: No matter who is put on a cross, he is still a human being and the cross is bad enough without splinters to make it worse.

Jesus: You know what I like most about working with you, Dad? It's like working with God in the carpenter's workshop.